"A fun and easy read, *The Bohemian Guide to Urban Cycling* is an insightful personal look into Portland's cycling culture."

Mia Kohout
CEO & Editor-in-Chief
Momentum Mag

"For a bicycling enthusiast, Portland is a special place—a pioneer not only in creating an extensive cycling infrastructure, but also in generating a supportive 'bohemian' counter-culture with cycling at its center. Sean Benesh's new book deftly introduces the reader to the nooks and crannies of this culture. However, Benesh is more than an aficionado for all things *Portlandia*; he is also a keen observer of the shadow side of 21st century American urban life—particularly the twin forces of gentrification and racial inequity that trouble Portland as well as other cities. In the end, his book is a guide not for hipster-wannabes, but rather for those whose imagination is fired by a passion for justice, and who can envision bicycling as a way to bring such justice into being."

Mark VanderSchaaf, PhD
City and Regional Planner
Minneapolis-Saint Paul, MN

"This book both celebrates Portland's unique, eclectic culture while offering deeper insight into the formation of this bohemian cycling culture. A thoroughly enjoyable and knowledgeable read!"

Jude Gerace
Sugar Wheel Works
Portland, Oregon

"I live in Long Beach, CA. On the exterior wall of our city hall, there is a written declaration, which states that Long Beach is 'the most bike friendly city in America.' While this may not yet be a reality, it's got its sights on Portland's crown, the laboratory setting for this book. Sean's passion for the people and places of his city fuels him to dive into one of the best ways to move in a city: urban cycling. As an ethnic bohemian, coffee loving, single-speed riding, and all around urban-nerd, he explores bicycling tribes with the embedded curiosity of a cultural anthropologist. If you want to embark on a life-long ride as a bohemian urban cyclist, this book is a great place to start."

Steven A. Chaparro
Visioneering Studios

"If the city we now know as Portland were destroyed in a catastrophe and its inhabitants scattered across the earth, I hope the exiles would spread their values and lifestyle to so many people that one day the world would forget the origin of the word 'Portlander' and instead know only that it refers to people everywhere who value joy above speed, discovery above wealth, and reasonably priced beers above razors. And if that ever happened, and if historians were later trying to piece together what it was like to be a real Portlander, I would recommend that those historians read this book."

Michael Andersen
Staff Writer
People for Bikes

"*The Bohemian Guide to Urban Cycling* documents the rise of the humble bicycle, from the counterculture into the mainstream, and the implications that has on the way we design and experience North American cities. Dr. Benesh truly understands the challenge of normalizing cycling for transportation, explaining that it's no longer about recruiting 'cyclists,' but rather getting regular 'people on bikes,' using lifestyle marketing techniques perfected by the automobile industry. A concise, informative, and entertaining read."

Chris Bruntlett
Modacity Founder
Bicycle Urbanist

"A concise and entertaining discourse on what it means to be an urban cyclist today. Sean provides a needed gloss on why bikes really matter to cities of the 21st century."

Charles R. Wolfe
Author, *Urbanism Without Effort*
Seattle Land Use and Environmental Attorney

The Bohemian Guide to Urban Cycling

SEAN BENESH

Urban Loft Publishers | Portland, Oregon

The Bohemian Guide to Urban Cycling

Urban Loft Publishers
2034 NE 40th Avenue #414
Portland, OR 97212
www.theurbanloft.org

ISBN-13: 978-0692289808
ISBN-10: 0692289801

Made in the U.S.A.

To all of you urban cowboys and cowgirls who daily mount your steel (or aluminum ... or carbon) steeds and pedal throughout the streets of the city.

Contents

Preface

I'm a bona fide book nerd. I own a lot of books and I read a lot. Most of the time I have my nose in a book whether it's a paperback or a Kindle version. Or it could be even a magazine. Usually as I grow interested in a topic I end up scouring Amazon and buying and reading books until I've had my fill and move on. Many of the topics and ideas found in this book have been germinating for years now and I have read lots on the subjects discussed here, from city cycling to bohemians to gentrification and so much more.

Usually in the preface authors attempt to wax eloquently about the creative impulses that led them to pour countless hours into writing the book that you're about to dive into. I often think that books emerge from an ongoing inner angst or urge to explore a topic in greater depth. That may be less true for works of fiction, but it's certainly true for non-fiction. I have read a lot of books on the topic of city cycling and most have been outstanding and helpful. So why then would the world need another?

We all write from a certain angle. That's to say, there can be ten authors all writing on the same subject but each of their books would be completely different. Sure, there's bound to be some overlap, but there would be something about each book to make it distinct. With that in mind I wanted to add my own voice into the mix on urban cycling. Not because I've written the definitive work on the subject, but I believe that my own perspective will help move the conversation forward as North American cities continue to push hard to become more bikeable and bike-friendly.

I have structured the book in two parts. The first eight chapters are more or less foundational issues and *how-to's*. From bohemians to mobility to how to pick out a bike to ride in the city, which bike tribe to align with, and more. These are basically the essentials to get you moving when you think and dream and plan on becoming a legit "urban cyclist." Chapter 9 and following move beyond the how-to's to explore the "other side" of the urban cycling scene. The conversation moves from skinny-jeans-wearing hipsters to gentrification, equity, race, and bicycles. Lastly, there are subjects within this book that I have been writing and teaching on for years. With that in mind I snagged a few stories and examples that I have written about elsewhere because I felt they fit well the trajectory of the book.

My hope is that this will be a fun and light-hearted book but at the same time poke and prod some uncomfortable topics that can't be ignored in this urban petri dish that we live in and study. To that end I tried to make this book reading-*lite*, in other words, not too beefy or academic. I throw in footnotes from time to time but for the most part, this book is certainly a far cry from anything remotely academic.

Acknowledgements

There are several people who come to mind that I'd like to thank who helped shape, influence, and inform this conversation whether they realize it or not. I am always appreciative of the tireless work of Frank Stirk who pored over this manuscript. The countless hours he has spent not only on this book but on many of my other books has forged a special bond with us. He takes my clunky sentences and half-baked thoughts and helps them to become succinct and readable.

There are also many others on the cycling side of things who've helped inform this book. Whether it's random conversations or shared experiences, the unifying factor is that these have informed my own thinking about cycling in the city both as a lifestyle and as a mode of transportation. Paul Dixon is not only my "online mechanic" friend but we have a never-ending conversation thread going about bicycles ranging from urban cycling to mountain biking (enduro, of course) to tips and tricks I've gleaned from his years as a bike mechanic. Paul helps me from afar. He lets me email him photos of bike problems when I get stuck on a mechanical issue involving one of my bikes.

There are other continual conversations I have on social media with people who have helped me think things through whether they realize it or not. Mark Peach in Salt Lake City, Colby Henley in Tucson, and Kyle Blake in Ft. Worth have been extremely helpful. Thank you all.

Thank you as well, reader, for picking up this book. Sometimes it is scary being an author because when we put content out there for public consumption we are inadvertently letting people peer into our own lives through the sharing of stories, examples, and even painful experiences. There is a vulnerability to this. I am humbled and appreciative of your interest in these topics and book.

Introduction

Right now up on my bike stand at home I have a mid-80s Diamondback mountain bike. It is summer in Portland which means I can count on endless days of sunshine to be able to work on my bikes at home out on the patio. Without a garage the patio is my self-proclaimed "man-cave" despite the lack of anything resembling a man-cave ... no work bench, no surround-sound stereo system, no tools hanging on a peg board or anything like that. Just a fourth floor patio overlooking a busy bicycle thoroughfare with a high volume of pedestrian traffic.

I have a seemingly never-ending stream of bicycles that I am working on either for myself or for friends. I have become a magnet to help fix up old janky bikes for buddies which I love to do. To me there's nothing better than the smell of Simple Green or bike grease wafting in the air. As I work on bikes under the cover of sunshine I sometimes will pause, pick up my cup of coffee, and lean on the railing looking down on the intersection below buzzing with all kinds of activity and vibrancy. And yet I tend to notice only what is important to me ... bicycles.

Last week was the kick-off to Portland's love fest celebration of the bicycle called Pedalpalooza. The parade of bicycles on the opening night wound their way through our neighborhood and right through this intersection. As a family we stood out on the patio watching hundreds of cyclists happily cruise by. The diversity of the kinds of bikes was fun to behold and point out. "Look at *that* tall bike!" one of us would say. "Did you see that cute pug in a sidecar?" my youngest son would exclaim in excitement. So many bikes from clunky beater bikes to sleek fixies to tall bikes to city commuter bikes to carbon road bikes and everything in-between. Seemingly no two bikes were alike.

So how does one write about urban cycling? And from which vantage point? I can only write from the only perspective I know ... my own. I am not a mechanic although I am handy enough that most of the time I don't need to take my bike to the bike shop. I don't work in the bike industry although for six years I did work as a mountain biking and a city cycling guide. Even today I still lead an occasional city educational tour by bike, mostly for college students. Obviously this all goes into the crock pot of who I am because it informs and influences my own perspective.

But in essence my framework could be boiled down to this one essential ... I ride bikes. *I ride bikes.* I like bikes. There is literally not a day that goes by in which bicycles are not a part of my life whether it's pushing past the three or four sitting in our living room (I have a patient and amazing wife), to the one, two, or three on our patio at various stages of being worked on, or the two more downstairs in secured bike storage. I read city cycling and mountain bike magazines bikes all the time, I watch Youtube or Vimeo clips of epic mountain bike adventures, I ride my bike(s) pretty much daily, and of course I am always thinking about how to buy more bikes. I like bikes. I ride bikes.

Now, I am not an elitist. All of my bikes collectively probably don't cost as much as yours. I'm into good yet affordable bikes. I just want to ride. As Lance once said (before his fall from grace) ... *It's not about the bike.* And yet this book is about bikes. So where's the rub?

In my regular travels I have conversation after conversation with people looking to get into bicycling as a mode of transportation. Those who ride primarily for the exercise probably already do so, but there are a growing number of people who are interested in trying out bicycling as a way of life and an alternative to hopping in the car. More people, sick of the costs associated with owning a car and the hours spent on their daily commutes are looking for cheaper and healthier options.

In essence I wanted to write a book based on these numerous conversations with people asking me about singlespeeds and fenders and the other peripheral issues that arise when talking about urban cycling. Not only that, but I wanted to treat seriously the context of where we ride ... in the *city*. We are rooted in place, in a context. We don't have the luxury of divorcing ourselves from geography.

All of this provides the backdrop of an introduction to urban cycling. At the same time this book goes beyond simply bike fashion, different kinds of bikes, and more to helping us understand *where* we ride and the influences, changes, and happenings in cities that impact this conversation on urban cycling.

Ready? Let's get after this.

Chapter 1

Bohemian Rhapsody

Portland and bohemians go together like Portland and coffee or Portland and bicycles or Portland and beer ... they are synonymous. You can't talk about Portland without talking about its bohemian hipster culture. For a summer I worked as a cycling guide here and had the fun opportunity of taking a myriad of tourists on bicycle tours throughout the city. For them it was a crash course in all-things Portland ... which means that I *had* to talk about the bohemian scene here.

One of the first stops on our tours, whether the Historic Downtown Tour or the Brewery Tour, would be at the Willamette River waterfront next to Burnside Bridge. It is an essential stop because it helps orient visitors as to how Portland is laid out and how the bridge and the Willamette River are the markers of how the city is divided between the quadrants of SW, NW, NE, SE, and even N Portland. I had grown accustomed to talking about Portland's bohemian and hipster scene and even the nuances of difference between bohemians in NW Portland (The Pearl) compared with those in SE and so on. I would try in the straightest face that I could muster begin explaining the fashion difference between bohemians in each of the quadrants of Portland.

"You see," I'd quip, "Bohemians in SE Portland represent the classic motif of hipster fashion by donning the 'double cuff' roll on their skinny jeans whereas hipsters in NE Portland are pioneering a new way to roll their skinny jeans by going for the 'single cuff.'" People would begin taking notes until I'd start laughing. Portland certainly has a robust bohemian and hipster scene. Portland State University professor Charles Heying in his book *Brew to Bikes: Portland's Artisan Economy* writes, "Other cities have their bohemian districts, but Portland stands alone as an urban economy that has broadly embraced the artisan approach to living and working."[1] You see, while New York City has Williamsburg and Chicago has Wicker Park, in Portland this scene is not simply reserved to one district. It is city-wide.

This became evident to me on a recent trip to Salt Lake City. I decided not to rent a car but instead get around on light rail and the city's bike share program. The bike share was a great way to explore the relatively flat city (except where it started getting hilly near the University of Utah). On a bike tour I told my friend, "Take me to the most 'Portlandy' part of the city." So he did. It wasn't very Portlandy. There were a couple of blocks attempting to cultivate Salt Lake's version of Portland or Williamsburg or Wicker Park. A couple blocks. That trip confirmed Heying's observation ... Portland doesn't have a "scene" that is only the size of a few city blocks or a

---

[1] Heying, *Brew to Bikes*, 17.

district ... it is our *entire* city with varying degrees of "thickness."

So why the fascination with bohemians? In case you're wondering about me, yes I am a bohemian. In fact I am a true Bohemian. Let me explain. The title of this book is both tongue-in-cheek and somewhat misleading but more accurate than one may realize. When I say *The Bohemian Guide to Urban Cycling* what I am saying is this ... I am truly a bohemian ... not the small-"b" type, but the capital-"B" type. Ethnically, I am a bona fide Bohemian. When my people immigrated to the United states at the turn of the 20th century, they came from what was then called Bohemia, and is now part of the Czech Republic. But yes, there was once a country called Bohemia. Many people don't realize that, but I have come across some startling exceptions to the rule. I had one such experience following a mountain bike injury in Tucson.

For about a five-year stretch I worked as a mountain biking guide in Tucson. It was at an exclusive high-end destination spa that celebrities and the cream of society go and hang out at. Oprah on one of her shows gave all of the studio audience a free stay at this resort. Needless to say, it was a fun experience because you never knew who was going to show up for a hike or a mountain biking ride. People like Oprah, Jim Carey, Ben Stiller, Susan Sarandon, and others were enjoyable and gracious guests as we trekked or pedaled in the desert wilderness.

The mountain biking tours were by far my favorite. Everyday we would offer a certain level of bike ride, most often these were either beginner or intermediate types of trips. We'd take people out on mountain bike rides who had little to no experience, especially in a hostile environment such as a desert where everything either wants to sting you, poke you, bite you, or poison you. However, every now and then we'd get an elite athlete which meant for two or three hours we had the privilege of riding hard racking up miles of pristine single track just north of Tucson on the 50-Year trail system.

Sometimes if there were no sign-ups for our bike rides we would either hang out in the shop working on our fleet of bikes or we'd head out to do some trail maintenance which would become an excuse to get in a mountain bike ride. On one such day I was out on the trail with another guide and after our trail work we began our trip back to the shop to eat lunch and then head home. Mountain biking in the desert means there are plenty of obstacles, not only the kind that inflict pain, but others that are a pain ... namely sand. The last obstacle between the trail system and the resort property is a 30-to-50-feet-wide wash with thick sand. It would change every time there was a flash flood.

The key to riding across this particular wash is to muster as much speed as you can in the approach so you can shoot across it (almost like gliding). Usually about three-quarters of the way across you'd start getting bogged down which means you're pedaling like mad to make it. It was at this moment that it all went wrong for me ...

As I started hammering on the pedals my right foot became unclipped and shot out. It hit the front tire and then was ejected back to the front chain rings. I was pedaling from the middle chain ring. I had just bought a new set of chain rings. They were sharp. Razor sharp. My right leg somehow got wedged between the front chain ring and the front tire ...

and all the while my left leg was still pedaling. I was sliced right open. Filleted. I opened up a six-inch-long gash along my Achilles tendon above my heel and up. It was a clean cut thanks to my new chain ring. I could see all the way to my tendon.

I was bracing myself for the pain, but it never came. Was I in shock? I did what any sensible mountain biker did ... I rode back to the shop which was still a mile away, took pictures, and then got a ride from the other guide to urgent care. I hobbled in bleeding all over the place like a stuck pig. As I was checking in and filling out paperwork the older dude behind the counter, as soon as I told him my last name, said excitedly out loud ... "Benesh? You're a BENESH? You're a Bohemian!" "Um, yeah," I said not knowing where in the heck this was going. He then proceeded to tell me about the famous (or infamous) Edvard Beneš (sounds like Benesh; immigrants to the U.S. added the "h.") who was president of Czechoslovakia during the 1930s and 40s. Edvard was a native of Bohemia.

After the doctor sewed my leg up and as I was hobbling out on crutches this same guy yelled across the room (in front of 30 patients) saying ... "Have a good day B-E-N-E-S-H!" I walked out thinking about my Bohemian roots and who this Edvard dude was.

Most people don't know about capital-"B" Bohemians, only the small-"b" skinny-jeans-wearing types. Two things happened in the desert on that day. First, I was reminded again of my roots. You see, the ironic thing about writing a book on urban cycling is that I was born and raised in Iowa. Yes, I-O-W-A. A place known more for corn and wrestling than it is for urban cycling. The part of the state I grew up in was settled by Bohemian immigrants. My grandparents on my Dad's side were still 100 percent Bohemian, as was my Dad. My Mom wasn't which means I'm 50 percent Bohemian. It was an agricultural community. I remember as a child going to Czech polka dances at the town hall in Chelsea with my grandparents or road-tripping on the back roads with my Dad as he listened to polka on the radio.

The second thing that happened on that day in the desert was my decision never to be filleted like that again. With three chain rings on the front most often I'd ride on the middle chain ring which of course left the large (new) chain ring on the front exposed with those sharp teeth and I DID NOT want to be sliced and diced again. That began the process of converting to ride singlespeed bikes. First it was singlespeed mountain bikes (with a bash guard for extra measure) and then I crossed over to riding singlespeed road bikes ... not fixies, mind you, but straight-up singlespeed speeds (I like to coast at times).

So how did we get from capital-"B" bohemians who didn't wear skinny jeans to the small-"b" kind like we have *ad nauseum* here in Portland? How did we transition from a ethnic group or nationality to a term used to describe today's urban hipsters and artists? According to the ever-oh-so-accurate *Urban Dictionary*, a bohemian is "somebody who leads an alternative lifestyle, they are not hippies because they can have an extremely wide range of different tastes in music, fashion, art, literature, etc. They are usually very creative people. They are above all optimists, even if they can be very cynical too (it does make sense ... sort of). They like wearing a mixture of weird clothes and mix different fashions together just for the heck of it. They like weed. Generally very laid back and relaxed."[2] This is a far cry from the ethnic Bohemian farmers of eastern Europe. So how did we get from the culture and inhabitants of the now-defunct Bohemia to the hipsters of today?

In his book *Neo-Bohemia*, Richard Lloyd explains, "In Paris in the nineteenth century, the term 'bohemia' evolved into both an ethnic designation, including the remnants of this defunct state scattered throughout Europe, and a more general epithet synonymous with gypsy and beggar."[3] These Bohemians began scattering throughout European cities and were considered a seedy lot. Over time the term "Bohemian" began to become increasingly synonymous not only with a certain ethnicity, but also more or less with a lifestyle grouping. In the *Westminster Review* in 1862, we read of these emerging urbanites. "The term 'Bohemian' has come to be very commonly accepted in our day as the description of a certain kind of literary gipsey [*sic*], no matter in what language he speaks, or what city he inhabits ... A Bohemian is simply an artist or littérateur who, consciously or unconsciously, secedes from conventionality in life and in art."[4]

The process of industrialization had an effect on these wandering Bohemians. Lloyd goes on the explain, "Potential creators were pulled to the metropolis by the centripetal forces also drawing peasants from the countryside. Too numerous to

---

[2] Urban Dictionary LLC, "Bohemian."

[3] Lloyd, *Neo-Bohemia*, 52.

[4] Harper, "Bohemian."

be absorbed by the professions and ill-suited by disposition to the sweatshops, those who would constitute the citizenry of bohemia settled into the low-rent districts of the city to ply their self-appointed trades."[5] That last sentence is key to our understanding of how we get to the small-"b" bohemians of today and eventually to the conversation about urban cycling.

Now we can begin to see the evolution ... seedy, rowdy, ornery, artistic, littérateur, urban, and swimming against the culture mainstream. *Wikipedia* defines Bohemianism as, "The practice of an unconventional lifestyle, often in the company of like-minded people, with few permanent ties, involving musical, artistic or literary pursuits. In this context, Bohemians can be wanderers, adventurers, or vagabonds."[6] Fast forwarding the storyline to more recent memory, we can begin to see the origins of how we got to today's bohemians and hipsters. One last quote from Lloyd helps paint the picture of how this bohemian lifestyle and culture arrived in this country. "In the United States, bohemia materialized most prominently at the turn of the twentieth century in the New York district of Greenwich Village, an avant-garde ghetto in a sea of cultural populism."[7]

Bohemianism begin spreading across American cities. Those who've adopted this lifestyle most often collected, as mentioned, in low-rent (think: cheap) districts in cities. Known for their flare for all things counter-cultural and a

---

[5] *Neo-Bohemia*, 53.

[6] Wikimedia Foundation Inc., "Bohemianism."

[7] *Neo-Bohemia*, 57.

progressive fashion sense, bohemians carved out a way of life in some now-famous districts ... Greenwich Village, Wicker Park, etc. Constantly looking for cheap places to live it is no wonder why bohemians in the truest sense were considered pioneer gentrifiers even though that label may not stick too well since they were hardly middle-class. Instead they gravitated towards neighborhoods and districts in the city that were the most affordable. As cities in the course of the 20th century shed their industrial-era factories and suburbanization grew, in its wake was left many empty warehouses and defunct factories ... prime real estate for the avant-garde bohemians. So they moved in.

Bohemians were the forerunners of urban renewal and other movements back to the city such as loft living. Lofts are not new and neither is this notion of loft living, but in the grand scheme of things they are relatively new. They began to proliferate in the 1970s. Up until then there was nothing very appealing about living in an old warehouse or closed-down factory. Sharon Zukin explains:

> Until the 1970s, living in a loft was considered neither chic nor comfortable—if the possibility was considered at all. Making a home in a factory district clearly contradicted the dominant middle-class ideas of "home" and "factory," as well as the separate work environments of family and work on which these ideas were based. Since the 1950s, suburbia had so dominated popular images of the American home that it was almost impossible to imagine how anyone could conceive the desire to move downtown into a former sweatshop or printing plant.[8]

---

[8] Zukin, "The Creation of a 'Loft Lifestyle,'" 175.

Somewhere along the way the urban fabric of cities began changing along with how people viewed cities. Space does not allow within the scope of this book to go into a lot of detail, but it should be noted the Industrial Revolution created certain factors that made cities unpleasant and unsavory, namely (a) rapid urbanization which meant overcrowding, and (b) the close proximity between factory and home. Given the lack of sustainability practices in cities, factories with belching smokestacks plus cramped housing minus cleanliness and sustainable practices created gritty, dirty cities. No wonder people were not keen on living in old factories and loft living was not on people's minds until the industrial city began to fade, leaving empty buildings in its wake.

However, the key changes taking place which were reshaping the cultural preferences for Americans included a change in lofts themselves as well as a change in middle-class consumption patterns.[9] This was all part of the larger reshaping of cities. Never mind that part of it is a somewhat naive romanticizing of the past; as Zukin quips, "Only people who do not know the steam and sweat factory can find industrial space romantic or interesting."[10] Nonetheless, the continued growing appeal for loft living is an identification with the past and a desire for a new and even chic way to live. That places bohemians squarely in the middle of this conversation.

---

[9] Ibid.

[10] Ibid., 176.

Lofts are appealing to many and not simply young 20-something hipsters. As lofts become even more fashionable and desirable they also become expensive and exclusive. Usually when one thinks initially of loft living the images conjured up are of starving artists squatting in an open former industrial building with a bed, a lamp, and design table amidst ten thousand square feet of emptiness that gets bone-chilling cold in the winter due to a lack of heat or any basic amenities. The skinny-jeans-wearing artist in a beret and scarf throws outlaw-type raves in his place on the weekends which is known locally and inside the scene as "the spot."

Fast forward to today and many loft residents are retired baby boomers who sold their massive suburban homes to move into and experience urban life as empty nesters (which I applaud). Just this morning while sitting in one of my favorite local coffee shops I watched a man in his late 60s walk in wearing cycling shoes, a bike helmet, and a fashionable Chrome messenger bag slung over his shoulder. Not everyone who lives in the Pearl District or the inner-city neighborhoods are poor hipsters and bohemians.

Lastly, the allure of loft living has to do with the building design and architecture of yesteryear.

> Loft living is part of a larger modern quest for authenticity. Old buildings and old neighborhoods are "authentic" in a way that new construction and new communities are not. They have an identity that comes from years of continuous use, and an individuality that creates a sense of "place" instead of "space." They are "New York" rather than "California," or "San Francisco" rather than "Los Angeles." Such places grow organically, not spasmodically. Because they are here today *and* tomorrow,

they provide landmarks for the mind as well as the senses. In a world that changes moment by moment, anchoring the self to old places is a way of coping with the "continuous past." So loft living rejects functionalism, Le Corbusier, and the severe idealism of form that modern architecture represents.[11]

It can be argued that bohemians and hipsters were the early adopters of many things such as fashion, art, lifestyle, and so on. As I mentioned earlier, bohemians also can be viewed as pioneer gentrifiers as they are the ones who moved back into degraded inner-city neighborhoods looking for not only a cheap place to live, but also the cultural experience of living in marginalized and ethnic enclaves. One of their goals is to keep ahead of the pace of society as a whole. Usually by the time a trend has gone mainstream bohemians have already moved on to something else. A cruise around Portland by bike reveals what American society as a whole will embrace as art, fashion, music, and culture five to ten years from now. This is much to their own angst and chagrin ... that what was once counter-cultural and off the beaten path has now been packaged and sold at Target.

What about urban cycling?

Same rules apply. I'll get into this later, but one of the key separation points between bicycling for utilitarian purposes versus recreational is that for the former group it is about getting from Point A to Point B, which means there are a lot of crappy bikes on the road. You see, if you're a poor bohemian you don't necessarily have the dough to drop $1,000 to $2,000 on a sweet Italian fixie. Instead you're grabbing whatever

[11] Ibid., 181.

moves, maybe putting road slicks on a mountain bike, some fenders, and you're off on the city streets. That does not diminish the desire to own nice bikes or to ride something fashionable, but we're talking early adopters now. That also explains the love for fixies ... no brakes, no components, no hype ... just a solid cheap bike.

The urban bohemians and hipsters of yesteryear rode bikes when it was neither cool nor fashionable nor even safe. Often they rode on city streets that had little to no bicycle facilities or infrastructure. This is now getting into the stuff of legends; you can still find old grainy video footage of alley cat races through cities like New York. They rode fixies because they were minimalistic, cheaper, easier to maintain, and perfect for bike messengers and the like. Since converting to singlespeed ten years ago I embraced the freedom it provides. I don't have to keep up with the arms race of buying new components that are always evolving and becoming more expensive. Also, I don't have to worry about knocking my derailleur out of whack because there is less to break and less that can go wrong.

I would be remiss if I didn't update the conversation on all things bohemian. You see, bohemians at the turn of the 20th century were different from the bohemians of the 1970s compared with the bohemians of today. They're no longer an avant-garde marginalized and fringe group. Bohemians are mainstream. Hipsters are everywhere ... from the suburbs of Nashville to Cedar Falls, Iowa, to Boise, Idaho, to Waco, Texas.

Bohemianism is about the arts, fashion, literature, and culture-making as a way of life. This makes it an economic conversation and we could spend a lot of time talking about the shift from Fordism to Post-Fordism, but needless to say, we're in a post-industrial economy. What that means is that as manufacturing jobs were either outsourced, computerized, or halted altogether, in its place rose not only the service sector ... but also the creative economy, and thus the rise of Richard Florida's "creative class."

So who is this nebulous creative class? Florida writes, "The distinguishing characteristic of the Creative Class is that its members engage in work whose function is to 'create meaningful new forms' define the Creative Class as consisting of two components. The Super-Creative Core of this new class includes scientists and engineers, university professors, poets and novelists, artists, entertainers, actors, designers and architects, as well as the thought leadership of modern society: nonfiction writers, editors, cultural figures, think-tank researchers, analysts and other opinion-makers. Whether they are software programmers or engineers, architects or filmmakers, they fully engage in the creative process."[12] Within this creative class (bohemians, artisans, hipsters) there is also a larger overarching category: "Beyond this core group, the Creative Class also includes 'creative professionals' who work in a wide range of knowledge-intensive industries such as high-tech sectors, financial services, the legal and health care professions, and business management. These people engage in creative problem solving, drawing on complex bodies of knowledge to solve specific problems. Doing so typically

---

[12] Florida, *The Rise of the Creative Class*, 69.

requires a high degree of formal education and thus a high level of human capital."[13]

In other words, the bohemians of today are no longer poor per se. They are squarely middle class ... which means they have the dough to drop $2,000 on a sweet Italian fixie. Even in Portland the bohemian culture has shifted dramatically over the last twenty years ... from fringe to mainstream. As I sit here at Heart Coffee on Burnside this morning a few things become abundantly clear: (1) This is a great place to watch hipsters and bohemians in their natural habitat. And (2) a number of the bikes parked out front are *not* cheap.

So now what? We have a growing population of bohemians / hipsters / creative class who are moving into urban neighborhoods, hopping in the saddle, and bicycling around for transportation. What's there left to say?

---

[13] Ibid.

Sean Benesh

Chapter 2

Mobility and Transportation

Not all cities are created equally. Admittedly living in Portland is in many ways like living in a parallel universe or an utopian paradise ... well, minus the eight months of rain. We have an amazing food scene, an incredible local beer scene, top-tier coffee roasters seemingly on every corner, and so much more. For those who love the bicycling scene we're the closest thing on this continent to Amsterdam or Copenhagen (apart from Montréal). Obviously there are other great bicycle cities that have even a higher percentage of cyclists like Davis or Boulder, but it all comes together in Portland. It also helps that we're a larger city known for other urban innovations. Add to that we are one of the epicenters of the bicycle industry. So if you're into bikes then either you end up moving here or you at least come to check out the scene.

I have heard from many people who visited Portland that they felt a kind of culture shock, especially among those from conservative towns and cities in the Midwest or South. They came away from their Portland experience overwhelmed by our quirky city. Many said how paralyzed they felt driving here because of all the bicyclists zipping around the city. They were not used to sharing the road with people riding bikes and were deathly afraid of hitting someone. Truth be told, that kind of culture shock is often *reversed* when we Portlanders visit other cities ... particularly the Sunbelt cities.

Now before I dive into my diatribe, let me be upfront and say ... I'm not a hater. Also, I have been impressed with cities ranging from Houston to Tucson to Phoenix to Salt Lake City which are aggressively going after improving their bicycle infrastructure. This is not about Portland snobbery and elitism. It's simply that when you live and bike around Portland you grow so accustomed to our bicycle facilities that when you visit other cities it is a shock. But that is rapidly changing.

I always like to quote Harvard economist Edward Glaeser in his book *Triumph of the City* who writes, "Transportation technologies have always determined urban form."[1] This fits perfectly with Jeff Speck's comment in his book *Walkable City*, that "the way we move largely determines the way we live."[2] These twin quotes are very telling when it comes to interpreting what we see and experience in our own city or when we visit other cities.

According to Glaeser one of the best interpretive tools in understanding what a city values and how it grew, expanded, and the point in history when all of that took place is in regards to the evolving transportation technologies combined with the changing cultural values of Americans. City centers built before the advent of the personal auto tend to be more

[1] Glaeser, *Triumph of the City*, 12.

[2] Speck, *Walkable City*, 55.

compact, dense, and walkable. As we transitioned from pedestrian-oriented travel to electric streetcars cities developed the technologies to expand outwards.

As an example, I live in what had been a "streetcar suburb" at the turn of the 20th century. A mere three miles outside the central business district, the streetcar line allowed for the city to expand outward. As a result the density lessened. However, after World War II as more and more Americans bought cars, this quickly gave way to auto-oriented planning which allowed the city to expand further outward more rapidly, and at even lower densities. For newer cities (or ones that went through a population boom at the same time more people began driving cars) with ample room to expand (e.g., in the Sunbelt cities) it allowed them to sprawl as streets were configured for auto usage.

No conspiracy theories here. When I visit cities like Tucson or Salt Lake City or Dallas I keep this in mind as I am overwhelmed by their massive arterials. On that same trip to Salt Lake City that I mentioned earlier one of the first things I noticed as I walked and bicycled around downtown and the central city neighborhoods was how insanely wide the roads were. Not the most pedestrian-friendly environment. However, these same roads also give planners almost a blank slate to propose such bicycle-related facilities as cycle tracks and road diets. The plan is to have them in place in the next few years. So what does this all mean?

If Glaeser is correct in his notion that transportation technologies have always affected or determined urban form then it is revealing about why and how our cities are laid out the way they are. It doesn't take a rocket scientist (or transportation planner or traffic engineer) to realize that cities and districts within cities that we love the most are usually older, chaordic, mixed-use, walkable, bikeable, active, and vibrant, and together create an overall pleasant experience. If you were to show me pictures from one of your recent trips to a city that you visited what would I see? Probably photos of you walking around some cool historic district soaking in the vibrant walkable urbanism as you long for a yesteryear when cities were all like this. Am I right?

Last fall I took a trip to Montréal. It was my first time there and Montréal was one of the cities I most wanted to visit not only for its Québécois culture (and poutine), but also for its BIXI bike share, its grand historic architecture, and of course the Molson Stadium where the Montréal Alouettes play. On the third day I was with a group of friends walking around Vieux-Montréal (Old Montréal). We were basking in the sites, sounds, and smells of this beautiful historic district. Of course the thing that caught my eye was a bike shop. The owner was outside bringing in his fleet of rental bikes for the evening. I stopped and chatted with him for a moment hoping to learn more about cycling in Montréal, how the bike share impacts his business, and what bike commuting in winter is like. It was a brief conversation. But I looked around and my friends were gone. Gone. I had no way of getting hold of them. The only thing I knew was a rough estimation of when and where we were going to meet up for dinner. It was in the same area so I didn't fret too much. Instead I wandered the streets of Old Montréal alone for several hours. It was epic.

One of the reasons why people love walking or bicycling around this part of the city is because it dates back to the 17th century. Since it was built long before the auto it had to accommodate people who got around on foot or by horse. That meant the streets are more narrow and the buildings are compact. We like that. We long for that. Buildings are not set back fifty yards from the street but instead come right up to it. This creates a rich environment for walking and bicycling. Contrast that experience with many Sunbelt cities that saw explosive grow after World War II. The result is quite the opposite of Old Montréal. Again, Gleaser provides an interpretive template for us to begin understanding why cities are the way they are. And what about Speck's quote?

Speck's notion of "the way we move largely determines the way we live" is pretty telling. Think about it. How we move around, how we travel, how we get from Point A to Point B, determines much of our lifestyle. No quote has better captured some of the most prominent dynamics of city life today. So, how do *you* get around? Be honest. Your answer reveals a lot. Again, this isn't to berate or brow-beat people, but sometimes honest assessments are helpful.

When I think of the last three cities I have lived in there is little doubt that the way I moved around had a big impact. My mode of transportation would be like looking into the proverbial crystal ball to see what my lifestyle was like. Obviously there were and are many other factors that contributed to my lifestyle choices, but the impact that transportation choices (or the lack thereof) have on our lives is enormous. Again, I feel like I need to reiterate continuously that I harbor no grand conspiracy theories about anyone's transportation mode of choice, nor do I hold to the notion that there is some inter-governmental global organization plotting ways to get us to consume more fossil fuels and drive large SUV's with kickin' subwoofers and satellite radio. But as Speck notes, I do believe that the way we move determines, dictates, and influences the way that we live.

For many years I lived the suburban lifestyle in the sprawling Sunbelt city of Tucson. It wasn't on the level of *The Truman Show*, but we lived in a sub-development where every fourth or fifth home was the same and the neighborhood shared the same color palette. At that point in my life, all I had known was an auto-dependent lifestyle. Growing up in small-town Iowa, from the moment I turned sixteen I had driven a car everywhere for everything. I really had little choice based upon where I lived because it was planned with the car in mind. The same was true for my subdivision and suburb. It is not that I harbored any resentments or hated it, it was simply part of my life.

My office was twenty-four miles away and it would take anywhere from forty-five minutes to an hour to get there. Again, nothing dubious ever crossed my mind. I simply made the drive and enjoyed listening to sports talk radio on the way. Besides, during eight months of Tucson summer I couldn't fathom getting around any other way since air conditioning seemed non-negotiable. All during this time I moonlighted as a mountain biking guide where I would drive to our guide office before we headed out on the trail. My drive of sixteen miles was actually one of the closest commutes compared to the other guides.

Towards the end of our time in Tucson when I was working on a doctorate focusing on various aspects of urban studies, urban renewal, and community development, my eyes began to open up to the urban dynamics I lived in. Being a cyclist (a mountain biker *only* at the time) I thought it'd be cool and novel to see if I could actually bike around for nearby trips. The problem was my part of the city was created for the car-lover and car-user. If I wanted to even use the bus it was a four-mile trip to get to the nearest bus stop. The closest coffee shop was a mile-long bike ride on a road with no bike lane and narrow gravel shoulders where cars drove fifty miles an hour. To head to the other coffee shop (Starbucks of course ... this was suburbia) it was a four-mile trip on similar road conditions. Not for the faint of heart. So I gave up. Looking back I would contend that the bicycle infrastructure in that part of the city was certainly not bike-friendly ... it was almost bike-deterrent. I lost. Sure I'd leave from my garage on my mountain bike and head for trails which I could do by following trails next to and in and through washes, but that was about it.

Tucson was a stark contrast to the next city that we lived in, Vancouver, British Columbia. Beyond the obvious differences like weather (rain? what is that?), culture (from the strong Hispanic culture and history in Tucson to the pervasive Asian influence in Vancouver), and most notably in terms of this book, the built environment of the city. Technically, we didn't live in Vancouver proper, but one of the city's suburbs, Burnaby. Now mind you, for those of you who've been to this world-class city you know that Burnaby is far from the stereotypical American suburb. It is decidedly urban. Calling Burnaby a typical suburb would be like calling Brooklyn a typical suburb.

41

We lived in Edmonds Town Centre, a rapidly growing "transit-oriented development." It was growing *up*, as in vertically. The skyline of our town centre had a more impressive skyline than Tucson with its numerous twenty-plus-story mixed-use residential towers. The neighborhood was anchored by Highgate Village. We lived two blocks from these towers. They filled the view from the kitchen window of our two-story apartment. It was a beautiful sight. The neighborhood was serviced by the Skytrain (light rail) and the innumerable bus lines that intersected the neighborhood. Through transit we could rather quickly get to most parts of Metro Vancouver.

We lived car-less. This was a huge adjustment from life in Tucson, but after the initial adjustment period we grew to thoroughly enjoy this experience. The schools had been set up to be walkable for children as the neighborhood catchments were very small. We lived two blocks from the elementary school. It wasn't always convenient but we began to enjoy our times as a family on the bus, the Skytrain, and the Seabus that would take us across the Burrard Inlet to North Vancouver. As a matter of fact, we enjoyed exploring the city this way, especially taking the Skytrain to the Waterfront Station downtown and hopping on the Seabus.

I didn't bicycle a whole lot to get around even though Vancouver is lauded as a bike-friendly city. Not so much in Burnaby. I still only had my mountain bike and a penchant to still be anti-roadie. From time to time I'd ride an hour up to the North Vancouver coffee shop my wife worked at to see her and hang out. My nobby tires were not the best for the road and I dreaded the day I would ever be labeled a "roadie." No thanks, I abhor tight-fitting Lycra and prefer the baggy clothes and disheveled look of a mountain biker. I had no fenders, no lights, just a desire to hang out with my wife on her breaks and drink epic coffee from JJ Bean and look out the windows of the coffee shop at the North Shore Mountains.

Our transition to Portland began seeing all of these disparate ideas and notions come to fruition. I had heard about Portland's bike-nutty culture and how it was held up as an American version of Amsterdam with loads of people riding bikes throughout the city. When we first landed in the city I was absolutely dumbfounded by how many cyclists were on the road. Sure, Vancouver has a reputation of being bike-friendly as well, but I didn't see much or experience it from Burnaby. In Portland wave after wave of cyclists passed by where we lived and I had to pinch myself. If there was ever an utopian society that I could create that synthesized good coffee and bikes, it would look a lot like Portland. The problem though was I knew my beloved singlespeed KHS soft-tail mountain bike was not going to cut it.

I had to become a roadie.

A roadie.

Really?

In form-fitting Lycra?

You mean becoming a bike snob where I'm always talking down to "others," constantly polishing my frame, and eating super healthy energy snacks?

Ugh.

As a singlespeed cross-country mountain bike rider I had the whole singlespeed thing down. I'm anti-gears (too much hassle). A month after arriving in Portland I went to a (cough) brand name national bike retailer. I am cheap. I mean, if I'm going to ride on the road I'm not dropping $3,000 on some carbon road bike that is lighter than a kitten. I wanted a rough high-tensile steel frame (or chromo) singlespeed road bike with cheap parts that I can swap out over time.

Bam.

Found one.

$220.

I was now a roadie, right? Nope, no way. Over time (I'll address bicycle fashion in a later chapter) I began to figure out my "look" when riding the streets of Portland on my singlespeed. I have replaced literally *all* of the parts of that bike by upgrading, including the frame twice. I have it dialed in to my preferences in terms of the gear ratio, the perfect stem / handlebar setup, saddle, and so on.

Portland is easy to get around in if you live in the central city. I say that because for the most part our suburbs are just like any other suburb, but if you're fortunate enough to live in the central city it is a bicyclist's paradise. Really. The city has favorable conditions for many urban dwellers to leave the car parked at home for most if not all trips.

In Vancouver we lived car-less and now in Portland we have a car (a gas-guzzling eight-cylinder SUV with heated seats and satellite radio), a scooter, and my bikes. For me, pretty much all of my trips in the city are by bike. I'm not a purist by any standard, nor do I suspect that you are either. I still enjoy cars and they certainly have their place. As an example, yesterday I was grateful to have a car in which to get to Cascade Locks which is a forty-five-minute drive into the Columbia Gorge from Portland. There is a fun little singletrack trail system (easyCLIMB) that I enjoy hitting up on occasion, especially when there are dry days in the winter. However, in the city I pretty much exclusively move around by bike.

For most of last year I commuted from my place in inner NE Portland to downtown on nearly a daily basis. From my apartment to where I needed to get to was four-and-a-half miles which took me fifteen to twenty minutes. It was a quick jaunt that was and is pretty straight-forward. Once I am at the Willamette River I join thousands of other cyclists riding across one of numerous bridges spanning the river. Every one of us has our favorite to ride across ... Steel Bridge, Burnside, Hawthorne, and so on. Most of the time I cruised across the Hawthorne. If you time it right, on the last Friday of the month is "Breakfast on the Bridges" where cyclists crossing the bridge are offered free coffee and donuts.

When I rode home at the end of the day (or when I still now travel into the downtown) I turned my fifteen to twenty minute ride into an hour ride by taking numerous different longer routes back home. Probably one of the most enjoyable parts is when I cross over or under one of the several freeways. I notice how insanely backed up the traffic usually is. If you're commuting by car from downtown Portland north on I-5 to cross the Columbia River into Vancouver, Washington, sometimes the traffic can be backed up for miles. Instead, I happily ride my bike and enjoy my commute. I am reminded of a post I saw recently on Facebook that read, "You are not stuck in traffic. You *are* traffic. Get out and ride a bike."

Like I mentioned, if you're into bikes then Portland is like a mini-utopian society. Even though we bemoan the eight-month-long rainy season it also acts as a deterrent otherwise we'd be the size of LA. It weeds out the weak. Even today, in mid-November, it is raining (surprise) and I'm sitting in a coffee shop (surprise) along North Williams which is a major bicycle corridor. Ristretto Roaster has become a home away from home for me. It is a great place to observe Portlanders in the groove of daily life ... coffee in the morning, beers in the afternoon (there are two local breweries across the street), and bikes all day. Even on a lousy day all of the bike parking out front is jammed with bikes snagging up the precious covered parking.

Periodically throughout the year I teach incoming groups about some of the urban dynamics shaping the city of Portland. Over several days we trek around the city by bike and public transit. We end up spending a whole day in this part of inner NE / N Portland addressing the correlating topics of bicycles, Portland's artisan economy, the creative class, and gentrification.

Numerous story lines collide at once along this stretch of road along North Williams Avenue. The topic and conversation of something seemingly benign like mobility and transportation is fraught with tension ... racial tension, socio-economic tension, and tension between bicyclists and motorists. However, at the same time it is a remarkable corridor catering to the growing number of bicyclists who use this thoroughfare in their commutes to and from Portland's central city. If you were to visit Portland to check out the bike scene, Portland's foodie scene, coffee scene, beer scene, artisan businesses, and the like ... I'd send you here.

Over the summer one of the coolest events that happens along North Williams is Rider Appreciation Day. Something like forty businesses band together to throw an appreciation party for bike commuters who use this corridor. Business after business set up tents, booths and stands, and gave out food, beer, soda, and swag. As I rode this route on this particular day it was humbling. I was taken aback hearing so many different people working the booths yelling out, "Thanks for riding!" It was a fun time. There was great food and live music. It certainly made this commute pretty special. It also made me incredibly grateful to live in a city like Portland.

I mentioned at the beginning of this chapter that not all cities are created equal. While there is certainly something special happening here in Portland, as I will point out next chapter, the momentum is picking up in cities across the nation to become more bikeable and bike-friendly. This ranges from conservative Midwest cities, to cities in the deep South, to major urban centers like New York and Chicago. If Portland hiccups we just may lose our status as "America's Bicycle Capital" (and in the eyes of many we already have).

Glaeser and Speck nailed it by pointing out that mobility and transportation impact much of urban life. They influence not only the built environment of the city, but also how we move around it. The conversation about urban cycling is a call for more and more people to get out and ride. Even if that means dropping the form-fitting Lycra and put on jeans, a wool jacket, and a hipster scarf as you hit the streets on your urban commuter bike. It just might catch on. We have to start somewhere.

Sean Benesh

Chapter 3

The Changing Landscape of Urban Cycling

More than any other place I have lived in, Portland gives you permission to simply be yourself. Those who visit from outside the area recognize this on their first day. I mean, have you seen what people wear? The first week after we moved here some giant dude came cruising by on his tall bike. He was rocking a kilt, was shirtless, and sported Dr. Seuss-like knee-high socks. From that day forward I didn't really care much how I dressed or what my hair look like. Of course, Portlanders have mastered the manufactured bed-head look (with gel). But there is something about Portland that gives you permission to simply be yourself which means when it comes to showing up for meetings, coffee or beers or whatever by bike, you're given a pass for helmet hair.

Ah yes, helmet hair.

I have to be honest here. I have now tried for several years to find the *right* hairstyle that is both "urban cool" and doable since I wear a bike helmet all the time. Well, not all the time. I don't wear one to bed. While I'm grateful to have crested the 40-year mark and still have a full mop of brown hair, to find the right kind of hairstyle that accommodates helmets is an art form. Unfortunately I've yet to master it. That probably explains why I wear a hat a lot of the time (like today). Maybe I shouldn't be so cocky that I have hair because if I was bald I'd have nothing to fuss over.

One of the factors that influences helmet hair is the style of helmet. Do you rock a road helmet? A more "city-specific" one like a Bern or a Nutcase? Mountain bike helmet? Wait, a mountain bike helmet? Really? Whew ... that's a no-no. While I'm not a *fashionista* one of the things you *don't* do is wear a mountain bike helmet in the city. I don't know why. It is simply one of the *unwritten rules* of urban cycling. You'd look like a tourist so please stop. Now if you must have a visor then wear a cycling cap underneath your helmet. Enough said. Of course I am only part joking because really any kind of helmet is essential. As I *just* typed this I looked over my shoulder in the coffee shop here and noticed someone with a $250 mountain bike helmet. Lime green too.

One of the common sights in Portland is showing up for a meeting, coffee or beers with a friend, work, or school and seeing a ton of others who, by their attire, you could tell they rode their bikes. There are the usual dead-giveaways like people carrying their helmets or, particularly true for Portland and the Pacific Northwest, waterproof messenger bags. I think I've seen just about all of the options for waterproof bags out there whether from Ortlieb, Mission, Chrome, North St., Black Star, SealLine, and so many more. Other indicators are the usual suspects with the right pant leg rolled up, cycling shoes, cycling-specific waterproof jackets, and of course helmet hair. But that is actually a good thing.

For cycling to become more mainstream it has to move beyond middle-age men in Lycra and into the more everyday usage of bikes. That bicycling would be as normative as driving cars, using public transit or walking. That means the more a city is accepting of people rolling into meetings or the grocery store with helmet hair or their right leg rolled up or heck, even just wearing a helmet *while* they're getting groceries, then we're moving forward in the right direction.

Lately I've noticed pushback from numerous blog sites and advocacy websites about the need to redefine terms and adopt new ones. You see, I'm *not* a cyclist even though I have used that term. I'm simply a dude who rides a bike. We normally don't self-identify by which mode of transportation we use. It'd be both a bit awkward and funny at the same time. "Hi, my name is Sean and I'm a transit-user." Or, "Yo, I'm a pedestrian." Even though "motorist" is a pretty common word in our vocabulary we still don't self-identify as a motorist. So why do we do it with "cyclist" or "bicyclist?"

I am first to admit that even though I may bristle at the term it is still an endearing term. Maybe that Jeff Speck quote ("the way we move determines the way we live") is also partly about identity. Heck, my Twitter handle is "mtbikerguy." I still identify heavily with *how* I get around and am especially proud to be a singlespeeder. I jokingly remark "before there were gears there were *real* men (or women)" or "gears are overrated." But I get the whole identity thing. Plus the only tattoo on my body is of a mountain bike wheel (26er, mind you). However, I also see the need for normalizing bicycling as a mode of transportation. To that end I am still simply a person who *uses* a bicycle to get around.

The more that we can normalize the use of bicycles in our culture the greater chance we have to see our ridership grow among people who use bikes for work trips, errands, and social outings. When I led bicycle tours in Portland one of the things that I worked hard at was to paint the picture of the bicycling scene here. Usually those on the tours were from all over the country and even from outside the U.S. I'd begin by explaining that pretty much every city has a bike "scene." I used Tucson as an example. Tucson is and has been known for its awesome bike scene. However, we need to unpack what that means.

When people talk about cycling in Tucson it is about road races, professional road teams that train there during the winter, or the mountain bike scene. It is *not* about bicycling as a mode of transportation (*yet* ... even though that is changing with a new bicycle infrastructure and great bike shops like Transit Cycles). In contrast, when I talk about Portland I do mention that we do have many of those elements ... road racing, mountain biking, and of course the rapidly growing cyclocross scene which gets bigger year after year. But what makes us different is the number of people who use bicycling as their primary mode of transportation.

Again, there are numerous other cities with a higher ridership than Portland. I just read an article about this in *BikePortland*. Usually these are smaller college towns like Boulder, Ft. Collins, Eugene, and so on. What makes Portland unique is that we are significantly larger than a college town of 65,000. There is a mass and a momentum here. This agglomeration of a bike culture and our growing bike-related industry means that this clustering effect spurs on more innovation and momentum, and wider cultural appeal. If you're getting around by bike in your city and it is only you, Chuck, Marge, and Billy, then you'll be derided as a bit eccentric or kooky. However, if you're one of a throng of tens of thousands of other cyclists then there is a girth to the whole scene and like an ion it continues to attract more and build energy. (Please don't hold me to the accuracy of any scientific examples.)

To that end the more people who shed the Lycra and wear fashionable clothes like we see in Europe the more we'll work towards normalizing bicycling for everyone. I'm not a hater of Lycra-clad roadies who wear outfits picked out to perfectly match their bikes (and personalities) and have all of the color-coordinated accessories. But when normal Joe and Joan see that it is intimidating. They initially begin to think that maybe biking would be fun, but then they realize that they don't have the body type that looks great in skin-tight Lycra. Nor do they have the extra pocket change to drop $3,500 on a carbon road bike. So they stay somewhat content with their Nissan Altima. But what if more and more bike commuters looked like you? Like me?

That is what makes places like Portland unique. Sure, we have our streamlined Lycra-loving commuters on high-end bikes with high-end outfits, but there are throngs of others who are *not* like that. For me there is nothing better than seeing guys in suits riding their bikes across Hawthorne bridge or moms hauling around two little munchkins in a cargo bike. That normalizes bicycling; it is inviting rather than repelling. Since my "office" most of the time is at either Ristretto or Heart I watch the revolving door of patrons coming in and out all morning. Many do arrive by bike wearing normal "everyday" clothes. Nothing out of the ordinary. Obviously when it rains here (which it does a lot) maybe they'll layer-up with rain gear, but for the most part many bicyclists (or *people on bikes*) here in the city simply wear normal clothes and deal with the occasional helmet hair or those red imprints on your forehead which is a dead give-away you've been wearing a helmet. No worries though, this is Portland.

There are several stats floating around not only in Portland but in bicycle planning and advocacy literature. The first one is that roughly sixty percent of the population, when it comes to bicycling, are "interested but concerned." The other stat, which isn't a stat, but more or less a frame of reference, is that when planning for bicycle facilities (bike lanes, cycle tracks, etc.) we should ask, "Would I be comfortable sending an eight-year-old or an eighty-year-old on this?" You see, one of the barriers to more people hopping on bicycles is not only comfort (as we just explored when it comes to clothing), but also feeling a level of comfort riding on our streets. This became apparent for me last summer.

I was working alongside a visiting scholar from Germany who was here to do research and write a book. We talked throughout the summer about family, life, research, writing, and of course ... bicycling. In her home city she has been bike commuting for decades. All of her commute routes are on separated and buffered cycle tracks. That means she is not riding on the same road as vehicular traffic. It is very comfortable and safe which is why you see so many people in various European cities riding bikes without helmets. However, life in Portland is a far cry for her home city.

She spent the summer here getting around by bike. She didn't have a car. Her commute entailed a ride from SE Portland, across the Hawthorne bridge, and into downtown. She said for the first few weeks it was very uncomfortable biking around Portland. She was so used to separated cycle tracks and now she was riding on higher speed roads with cars and buses whooshing by inches from her. Even though she was a confident rider with lots of experience, it was still a transition. I wonder how many other people feel that way? Well, if the sixty percent number really is accurate then we know that there is actually a large swath of city dwellers who'd actually enjoy bicycling around the city but who simply feel uncomfortable. That moves beyond people fretting about bulging out of form-fitting Lycra, but instead involves basic comfort and safety on the roads. Houston ... we have a problem. Actually, Portland ... we have a problem.

There is good news.

Over the past year I helped on a project where we worked with a cohort of cities looking to implement sustainability projects tied to (in most cases) a larger downtown revitalization plan. Part of that entailed reading through a slew of downtown revitalization plans as well as bicycle master plans. What was exciting (this is the good news) is that city after city from coast to coast were aggressively moving forward in implementing plans to expand their ridership. While Portland, when it comes to larger cities, is perched at the top (but not according to some), there are many other cities pushing hard to catch up. If we continue to stagnate with our ridership, who knows? Maybe we'll soon be passed by (which many claim has already happened).

Usually when we think of bike-friendly cities we think of the usual suspects ... Portland, San Francisco, Boulder, Minneapolis, Davis, etc. However, what was encouraging to see were all of the other "non-sexy" cities getting onboard with bicycle infrastructure ... from conservative Midwestern cities to conservative cities in the South, and everywhere else in between. It is exciting to see this. This continues to normalize bicycling as a way of life and a mode of transportation. I mean, if we can get Des Moines, Iowa, on board or Salt Lake City, Utah, or (insert seemingly conservative city here) then we're well on our way. This *is* good news!

That same the summer I was back home in the mother state (Iowa) for a family wedding. It is always great to be back. I have not lived in Iowa for a good twenty-plus years spending all of my time in larger cities out west. When I first started going back home to visit family I'd usually point out the "obvious" (with my west coast snobbery and elitism) cultural differences between Iowa and the west. I'd comment how backwards Iowa is and that they are not as refined and culturally savvy as places like Portland or San Francisco or Vancouver, B.C. However, over time I dropped that stupid attitude. I was wrong.

When I was standing in the Cedar Rapids airport waiting for my flight some young college dude came up to me and struck up a conversation about my shoes. I was totting my Ortlieb messenger bag and wearing Chrome shoes and we chatted about singlespeed bikes and my shoes. He lived in Iowa City and went to the University of Iowa. I was peppering him with questions about the bike scene there and was pleasantly surprised. You see, it is not just a Portland thing.

Even other places like Lincoln, Nebraska, have a growing and awesome bicycle infrastructure. As a Husker fan I was happy to hear they now offer free bike valet parking for home football games (I went to college in Nebraska). Bicycling is becoming more and more normalized from coast to coast. This is good news indeed.

Portland's percentage of people who use bicycles for work trips and errands has plateaued. This is while other cities (Chicago comes to mind with their aggressive move to install cycle tracks) are playing catch up and are moving swiftly. Sure, we may have a little head start but it is encouraging to see this growing momentum across the country. Many here continually banter around the question, "Why are we at a plateau?" Every now and then the conversation comes up on *BikePortland* and what is evident is that while there may be more than one answer, I believe there is something we can point to. It is that "8/80 principle." In other words, would I be comfortable sending an eight- or an eighty-year-old cycling down this street?

While other cities are moving straight towards cycle tracks we continue to add bike lanes and neighborhood greenways. Would you send an eight-year-old down a typical neighborhood greenway in Portland? Some say yes, some say no. Bike lanes? Whew ... probably not. Several ones come to mind that are well-used ... Broadway through downtown, North Williams, Hawthorne heading eastbound off the bridge, and even the newly re-striped SE Division. I would place myself in the company of a confident rider who doesn't mind mingling with traffic. But I don't find those routes necessarily pleasant or overly safe. Lots of congestion, lots of movement, lots of different things that could go wrong ... for an experienced rider let alone for a kid or a senior. If we want to see our numbers even crest the ten percent ridership across the city we need to make bicycling safer and more pleasant. That usually means some kind of separated bike facilities.

Portlanders can now throw tomatoes at me.

I want roads that I would be comfortable sending my children down. I don't believe that bicycling in cities should only be for the overly confident and the aggressive. Maybe that is why there is so much Lycra on the road. Lycra-clad riders tend to be good riders, confident riders, and aggressive in the sense they can take a lane when need be, accelerate to zip and zag through openings between cars, and have the fitness level to do all of the above. Maybe we need a new research tool or stat. Something along the lines that the number of Lycra-clad cyclists in proportion to the overall number of riders will tell us the real story of bicycle facilities. The higher the count the more tenuous the facilities. Conversely, the more people donning everyday clothes ... wools, cottons, overcoats, boots, dresses, or fedoras the safer and more accessible the bicycle facilities are for the general populace. Call it the *Fedora Principle.* Can you wear a fedora instead of a helmet on this bicycle facility and feel comfortable?

Now I'm not against bike lanes and I love and appreciate them. However, transportation planners and engineers don't need to build them for me because I'm not in the larger percentile of "interested but concerned." I'll ride anywhere including congested downtown streets where I'm zigging and zagging through tiny slots between cars. Bike lanes often provide the cheapest and easiest way to begin putting in *a lot* of bicycle facilities. It can be relatively easy compared to cycle tracks to simply put down some new paint. Maybe bike lanes are the gateway drug into more comprehensive facilities?

The encouraging news is to see so many cities teetering on the edge of starting to install new bicycle facilities. It is also neat to see the excitement of city planners and engineers when they tentatively put in their first bicycle facility. One of the cities that we worked with during the year is a typical sprawling Sunbelt city. While it has an architecturally rich downtown and walkable central city neighborhoods, most of its growth happened as auto usage was ramping up. That city, like most others, is more suburban than urban and as a result is car-dominated. In trying to move forward with downtown redevelopment it looked at numerous options. One of the projects it has been working on is to introduce bike share. We recently heard that it has secured initial capital to begin moving forward on this project. The problem is ... they don't even have a bike lane downtown.

The good news though is this city is now moving forward to install bicycle facilities downtown so that when the bike share opens people will have safer facilities to cycle on. Listen, I know that no city is perfect and even our most bike-friendly cities in the U.S. and Canada are considered substandard and subpar compared to our European counterparts, but at least we're trending in the right direction. We're a pioneering people. We are innovative, cutting-edge, and savvy. Sure we love our car but that is simply because it afforded us the opportunity to get from Point A to Point B as quickly as possible. Once we cross the threshold to where bicycles are more timely and efficient we'll be flocking over to them en masse. But it'll take time. The more acutely I am aware of this the more I have noticed our entrenched love affair with the auto. Even more so is the desperation car companies feel to keep us in love with their ever-oh-so-cool-fuel-efficient-comfortable mode of mobility. I now see car commercials as attempts to keep us driving and consuming the same as before. They still have a stranglehold on our collective imagination and as long as the auto is seen as a status symbol and linked to notions of freedom we'll be forever in their service. But bikes could indeed liberate us.

Again, I'm not a purist as I have a car and I enjoy it. I like my heated seats in the winter. But I've already proved that I *can* go car-free if I have to. Since those days north of the border in Vancouver we have gone from a car-free to a low-car-use lifestyle. Fortunately or unfortunately, much of it is tied to urban infrastructure and the ability to do this. Living at the intersection of bike routes that take me anywhere I want to go in the city is something I admit I take for granted. When I visit other cities this contrast is stark and evident. But the good news again is that more and more cities are moving in this direction so that those who want to go car-free or live a low-car-use lifestyle now can do so more easily. The landscape of urban cycling is changing before our eyes ...

Chapter 4

The Economic Benefits of Bicycle Facilities

As I mentioned in the Preface, one of my goals of this book is to steer away from an academic exposition of urban cycling replete with charts, citations, and footnotes *ad nauseam*. That would not be fun for any of us. Besides, when it comes to the topic of economic benefits of bicycle facilities or infrastructure there are a growing number of great works out there addressing this topic ranging from *City Cycling* by John Pucher and Ralph Buehler to *Bikenomics* by Elly Blue to blogs and everything in-between. There is a lot of great stuff out there as well as academic journals and web articles and blogs.

I wanted to address this subject by giving it some weight of viable information without getting lost in the minutia of geeky stats and nerdy charts. Besides, I hate numbers and I suck at math. When our kids hit fourth grade I had to tap-out when it came to helping them with their math homework. By the time they hit junior high I was a goner. Most of what follows in this chapter is my attempt to stay away from geekdom; at the same time I feel it's necessary to at least have some footnotes so it doesn't look like I'm pulling numbers and information out of my butt. I have one doctorate and well into working on my second so I feel like I know a thing or two about Nerdistan, but that is not the intention of this book.

Speaking of Nerdistan, the first time I ever seriously considered the economic benefits of bicycle facilities was actually in a PhD urban economics course. While we did not address bike facilities specifically we did hammer hard on agglomeration economies and location theory for businesses. Much of that conversation is directly tied to transportation, the ability to move goods around, and the importance of site selection for new businesses to maximize potential profit. That was super helpful as I watch the magic happen here in Portland in regards to our growing bicycle facilities, the impact of biking on local businesses, and even the larger trend of incoming dollars related to bicycle tourism throughout the state. As one who worked for a number of years in the tourism industry as a mountain biking, hiking, and cycling guide, I've seen first-hand its economic benefits.

Bicycling as a mode of transportation continues to gain momentum across the United States. That is something I am seeing and becoming more keenly aware of on a daily basis. I try to keep up by reading daily happenings on social media, articles, and blogs across the country. In Portland we're incredibly fortunate to have resources like *BikePortland* that keep us informed and engaged. I also experienced this first-hand as I have had countless conversations with friends in big and small cities alike throughout the U.S. and Canada asking me advice as they are looking to get into bicycling as a mode of transportation. I usually tell them I may not be the best person to help because if they truly listen to me they'll forgo gears and ride singlespeeds. But attitudes about bicycling are indeed changing and morphing.

More than simply a piece of recreational equipment, the bicycle is increasingly viewed as a viable mode of transportation for work trips and non-work trips alike. With the increase of cyclists on the road it is becoming clearer that they are having an economic impact in regards to the consumer choices and even location choices for businesses catering to the bicycling passersby or for their own bike-oriented employees. In this chapter I offer a *very* brief survey of some of the current literature surrounding this topic. Four categories emerge that will provide the trajectory and parameters of this survey: bicycle lanes and thoroughfares, the impacts of bike parking on local businesses, travel mode and consumer spending, and the influence of bike-friendly business in recruiting talent. Now before you hit your mental snooze button and check out until the next chapter, let me assure you that this is pretty legit stuff and well worth engaging in.

Much of the literature in this chapter stems from web-based articles detailing Portland's meteoric rise as a bike-friendly city. The reasoning behind this is that as Portland continues to help shape the conversation of bikeability in the U.S. there is a growing body of case studies and examples in this city to draw from. In other words, Portland can be viewed as a "living laboratory" to explore these related topics in the urban petri dish that the city presents. Lessons can in turn be gleaned from Portland and applied elsewhere. This is not to assert Portland has "arrived," but to point out the attempts and trends here in this city to move bicycling forward. There are indeed lots of both successes and epic failures.

The Value of Bicycle Lanes and Thoroughfares

Immediately noticeable in Portland are the innumerable streets with bike lanes hemming in most often the right side of streets. At times this takes the form of bike lanes and in other cases cycle tracks and neighborhood greenways. Pucher and Buehler note, "Lane lines are an effective means of channeling traffic, and because bike lanes are usually so narrow that motorists have no incentive to drive in them, they can provide bicyclists a reserved zone for riding despite the lack of a barrier from motor traffic."[1] (Doh! First footnote ... OK, so there will be ... cough ... a few in this chapter.) Particularly in the central city, what is evident are the growing number of commuters who travel to and from work on bicycles. Along with that are many others utilizing a bicycle for errands and other non-work trips such as to the grocery store, a favorite coffee shop or pub, and so on. People traveling by bicycles have begun impacting the local economy in such a way that businesses who find themselves along these routes are seeing an increase in bike-oriented customers.

There is a growing connection in the relationship between amenity- or service-oriented businesses and the proximity to bicycle thoroughfares. These kinds of businesses would include restaurants, coffee shops, pubs, boutiques, and the like. Michael Andersen, who writes for *BikePortland* and *People for Bikes,* has

---

[1] Pucher and Buehler, *City Cycling,* Loc. 2215.

written numerous articles that detail this trend. "Bikes, it turns out, seem to be a perfect way to get people to the few retail categories that are thriving in the age of mail-order everything: bars, restaurants and personal services. And in Portland, where an early investment in basic bikeways has made bikes a popular way to run errands, retailers are responding by snapping up storefronts with good bike exposure."[2]

Locally, an example of these changes taking place is North Williams Avenue (and North Vancouver Avenue) which carries thousands of bicyclist towards and away from Portland's downtown. (I have already mentioned this corridor). Over the past few years many of the businesses that have cropped up strategically cater to these pedal-powered consumers ranging from the Hopworks BikeBar, coffee shops (Ristretto Roasters), eateries, yoga studios, United Bicycle Institute, Portland Design Works (which makes accessories for bikes), and more. In one building alone there are three businesses owned and operated by women who cycle, a bike shop catering to women cyclists and their interests (fashion and otherwise ... which just moved up to Alberta Street), a bicycle frame builder, and a bicycle wheel builder. All of this bicycle traffic has influenced businesses here significantly.

Local Portland grocer New Seasons Market opened up a new store along North Williams Avenue in the middle of all the changes taking place along this corridor. Knowing the nature of this major bicycle thoroughfare, New Seasons actually has more bike parking than it does auto parking. "A

---

[2] Andersen, "Portland Retailers Swoop Into Storefronts Along Bikeways."

long row of bike racks has been installed on the east side of the New Seasons Market currently under construction on North Williams Avenue. While they take up only a small footprint of the overall site, the 30 staple racks have space for 60 bicycles—that's three more spaces than they've allocated for auto parking."[3] Momentum continues to pick up along this corridor and it is directly tied to the growing number of cyclists who use this route.

In the nearby Lloyd District a cycle track was recently put in along NE Multnomah. Cycle tracks afford comfortable riding for bicyclists and reduced traffic-related stress. "Most people find the quality of this experience far superior to riding in an environment in which one has to pay constant attention to traffic."[4] Already this has been viewed as a catalyst for redevelopment and creating a more vibrant and walkable urbanism. In his article "How Economic Growth Sold Portland Landlords on a Bikeway," Andersen lists the ways that this cycle track is impacting (and will continue to impact) development:

- Raising real estate values by quieting traffic. Raises visibility of a thoroughfare-type street, slows traffic down, increases pedestrian activity.
- Raising worker productivity. "Biking makes workers healthier," said Shannon Mayorga, executive assistant to Kaiser's vice president for human resources. "And physically separated bike lanes make workers bike."

---

[3] Maus, "New Seasons makes bike access a top priority at new Williams Ave location."

[4] *City Cycling*, Loc. 2176.

- Same roads, more capacity. After NE Multnomah was converted to cycle tracks there was a 1,000% increase in bicycles at Trailblazer games even in the winter.[5]

What is revealed both along NE Multnomah and North Williams is that bicycle traffic equates revenue for places like coffee shops, boutiques, pubs, and other specialty shops. "It's not just that a potential customer on a bike is just as valuable as the same potential customer in a car. It's that good bike access is disproportionately good for the core customers of bars and restaurants."[6] The thriving service sector benefits greatly from bicycles. Cycle tracks, bike lanes, and buffered protected bike lanes are good for business. A recent article highlights the benefits of protected bike lanes:

- Protected bike lanes increase retail visibility and volume. It turns out that when people use bikes for errands, they're the perfect kind of retail customer: the kind that comes back again and again. They spend as much per month as people who arrive in cars, require far less parking while they shop and are easier to lure off the street for an impulse visit.
- Protected bike lanes make workers healthier and more productive. From Philadelphia to Chicago to Portland, the story is the same: people go out of their way to use protected bike lanes. By drawing clear, safe barriers between auto and bike traffic, protected bike lanes get more people in the saddle "burning calories, clearing the mental cobwebs, and strengthening hearts, hips and lungs."

---

[5] Andersen, "How Economic Growth Sold Portland Landlords on a Bikeway."

[6] "Portland Retailers Swoop Into Storefronts Along Bikeways."

- Protected bike lanes make real estate more desirable. By calming traffic and creating an alternative to auto travel lanes, protected bike lanes help build the sort of neighborhoods that everyone enjoys walking around in. By extending the geographic range of non-car travel, bike lanes help urban neighborhoods develop without waiting years for new transit service to show up.
- Protected bike lanes help companies score talented workers. Workers of all ages, but especially young ones, increasingly prefer downtown jobs and nearby homes, the sort of lifestyles that make city life feel like city life. Because protected bike lanes make biking more comfortable and popular, they help companies locate downtown without breaking the bank on auto parking space, and allow workers to reach their desk the way they increasingly prefer: under their own power.[7]

The Impacts of Bike Parking for Local Businesses

Not only do bike lanes add benefit to local businesses, but so do bike corrals. What is a bike corral? "On-street Bicycle Parking Corrals make efficient use of the parking strip for bicycle parking in areas with high demand. Corrals typically have 6 to 12 bicycle racks in a row and can park 10 to 20 bicycles."[8] This uses space otherwise occupied by one to two cars. Bikeways are great ways to get people to businesses or at least pass them by, but having ample bike parking can be the difference between cyclists stopping or continuing on. Here are a couple of reminders from the article "3 Reasons Portland Retailers Have Embraced Bike Parking:"

---

[7] Andersen, "Here Are the 4 Ways Protected Bike Lanes Help Local Businesses."

[8] Portland Bureau of Transportation, "Bicycle Parking Corrals."

- Bike corrals make businesses more visible to everyone.
- Bike corrals improve the pedestrian environment.
- Bike corrals increase parking capacity.[9]

While certainly important, that is not the only consideration when installing bike parking in front of businesses. "But as more Americans use bikes for their daily errands, more retailers are thinking twice about their assumptions and realizing that once biking becomes easy and comfortable, busy neighborhoods are actually the perfect places to swap out auto parking."[10] There is a wait-list in Portland for businesses applying to have car parking removed in favor of installing bicycle parking in the form of bike corrals. Clearly, local businesses see the importance of bike parking over car parking, and they are willing to give up precious auto parking out front to cater to the needs and demands of bicycling consumers.

Clifton, Morrissey and Ritter explain this phenomenon: "Bicycle infrastructure can be controversial, particularly when on-street parking for motorists is removed to make way for bicycle lanes or parking. Typically, one or two automobile parking spaces can be converted to on-street parking for 20 to 40 bicycles."[11] Many business owners are seeing the economic benefits of giving up car parking to instead offer their

---

[9] Andersen, "3 Reasons Portland Retailers Have Embraced Bike Parking."

[10] Andersen, "Streets With Scarce Auto Parking Are the Best Places to Remove Auto Parking."

[11] Clifton, et al. "Catering to the Bicycling Market."

customers bike parking. Is it an idealistic notion or is there data to back up this conversion process?

Alison Lee in her Master's thesis *What is the Economic Contribution of Cyclists Compared to Car Drivers in Inner Suburban Melbourne's Shopping Strips?* noted that businesses have a higher return on investment when they forgo car parking for bike parking. In an analysis of the economic return on a parking spot in front of a business, Lee noted that in the end bicycling customers collectively will spend more than motorists in the same time period. A 140-square-foot parking space can hold either one car ($27 per hour parked, according to shopper behavior), or up to six bikes ($16.20 each per hour parked). It comes out to 19 cents per square foot: retail revenue per hour of occupied on-street auto parking, or 69 cents per square foot: retail revenue per hour of occupied bike parking.[12] "So it's not just out of the kindness of their hearts," Andersen writes, "that retailers in San Francisco, Minneapolis, Portland and Chicago are happily swapping on-street auto parking spaces for bike parking corrals, sometimes in the face of steep bureaucratic obstacles. For them, efficiently functioning neighborhoods are a matter of survival."[13]

On-street bike parking (bike corrals) does more than provide a space to park bicycles. It also helps bolster a vibrant sidewalk scene that is good for pedestrians. "Bars and restaurants have capitalized on this new infrastructure, which

---

[12] Lee, *What is the Economic Contribution of Cyclists Compared to Car Drivers in Inner Suburban Melbourne's Shopping Strips?*

[13] "Streets With Scarce Auto Parking Are the Best Places to Remove Auto Parking."

provides a buffer from moving traffic, by adding outdoor seating for sidewalk cafes. Because demand is so high, the city must place future corrals strategically and may institute a fee for installation."[14] All of this supports the same outcome of boosting localism which entails spending locally and supporting neighborhood businesses. Particularly for small businesses, gaining a better understanding of consumer choices and spending is essential not only for their survivability, but success.

Consumer Choices and Spending of Bicyclists

A perceived detriment of doing such things as removing auto parking in favor of bike corrals would be the fear of losing a valuable customer base, especially those who drive autos who could conceivably buy more due to their larger carrying capacity. This is a legitimate concern for businesses considering the possibility of foregoing a car parking spot in front of their business. However, recent research reveals the differences in spending between customers who arrive at businesses via bicycle, auto, or on foot (to build on what we just explored). As Clifton's key findings in *Examining Consumer Behavior and Travel Choices* reveal,

- When trip frequency is accounted for, the average monthly expenditures by customer modes of travel reveal that bicyclists, transit users and pedestrians are competitive consumers and, for all businesses except

---

[14] "Catering to the Bicycling Market."

supermarkets, spend more on average than those who drive.

- The built environment matters: We support previous literature and find that residential and employment density, the proximity to rail transit, and the amount of automobile and bicycle parking are all important in explaining the use of non-automobile modes. In particular, provision of bike parking and bike corrals are significant predictors of bike mode share at the establishment level.[15]

Writing for *The Atlantic Cities*, Emily Badger unpacks Clifton's findings in her article, "Cyclists and Pedestrians Can End Up Spending More Each Month Than Drivers." Badger notes, "bikers actually out-consumed drivers over the course of a month. True, they often spent less per visit. But cyclists and pedestrians in particular made more frequent trips (by their own estimation) to these restaurants, bars and convenience stores, and those receipts added up."[16] What this preliminary research reveals about consumer choices and spending by bicyclists and their economic impacts is that as a grouping they spend just as much as auto-users. One of the key points of difference is that shoppers traveling via bicycles are apt to stop more frequently.

What this highlights is that not only are bicyclists just as robust in their shopping as those who arrive in autos, but the fact bicyclists stop more frequently reveals one of the biggest incentives for businesses to offer on-street bike corrals: It is

---

[15] Clifton, *Examining Consumer Behavior and Travel Choices,* i.

[16] Badger, "Cyclists and Pedestrians Can End Up Spending More Each Month Than Drivers."

good for business. But what about the employees themselves? How do bike lanes and bike parking impact them?

The Influence of Bicycle Infrastructure in Recruiting Talent

The article "Good Bike Access Helps Score Greater Workers, Portland Firms Say" shows that bicycle access was influential in site selection for businesses relocating to parts of the city that have an ample bicycle infrastructure (bikeways and bike parking).

> In 2010, Jay Haladay, owner and CEO of Portland-based construction software firm Coaxis, invested $17 million to redevelop a central-city warehouse so his company could move from the side of a suburban highway to a location on central Portland's riverside bike loop. "This is all part of an effort to differentiate ourselves as an employer of choice," Haladay said. "You can't just throw benefits at people. You can't just have pizza at lunch." Bicycle access, Haladay said, lets a Portland employer play to its location's strengths. In this labor market, he's concluded, "any company that doesn't include it in its fabric of company culture is making a mistake."[17]

That is not the only consideration on the part of businesses relocating to districts and neighborhoods that are bike amenity-rich. Portland employers have indicated that bicycle commuting tends to boost productivity. But they've also found that locating in a bikeable part of the city is a great

---

[17] Andersen, "Good Bike Access Helps Score Greater Workers, Portland Firms Say."

tool for workers. "But more than anything, most agreed, the benefit of a bike-friendly worksite is simply that these days, valuable workers seem to prefer it."[18] It is an urban amenity that appeals to a growing number of workers.

Conclusion

Bicycles are beginning to reshape the landscape of American cities. As we've seen throughout this chapter, bicycling as a mode of transportation brings with it a certain amount of economic benefits ranging from the influence bike lanes have on adjacent businesses, the value of real estate, the recruitment of talent, and easier access for customers who ride bikes. The economic benefits of bike lanes, bike parking, and other bicycle facilities and infrastructure is positive for businesses who are trying to woo not only customers but top-notch employees as well.

Ok, enough of academic talk. Let's get back into the fun of urban cycling ... buying bikes.

---

[18] Ibid.

Chapter 5

Steeds of Choice and Those Who Ride Them

Since landing in Portland (believe it or not) I have read a good amount about the evolution of the American hipster. I mentioned already in Chapter 1 that I'm fascinated by the growth, transitioning, and transformation of this cultural milieu that I swim in on a daily basis. What fascinates me is that this conversation transcends merely what could be defined as hipster fashion and culture. In reality it is part of a larger economic movement that is reorienting cities on the local as well as global scale.

One aspect of hipsterdom that is fun to watch (again, I certainly do not classify myself as one) are the different breeds or subspecies of hipsters. There are a myriad of websites out there that act as field guides, like birding books, to help you identify the different *kinds* of hipsters not only here in Portland, but also in other cities. There could certainly be a hipster movie equivalent to *The Big Year* that instead of identifying bird species, looks for rare hipster subspecies.

When I was a mountain biking and hiking guide, while most of the other guides had almost memorized different bird books (since southern Arizona is a mecca of migrating birds), I struggled along. Sure I could point out some of the most obvious ones ... turkey vultures, quail, cactus wren, pterodactyl, but that was about it.

When it came to local knowledge of birds, flora, geology, and such, sometimes as guides we'd take advantage of those who came on our trips (usually Manhattanites) and play tricks on them. To them a bird was a bird and a rock was a rock. If it wasn't a taxi cab, a Chinese take-out restaurant, or a subway station, they were pretty much lost to grasp desert life in Arizona.

We'd weave tales of jackelopes or scare them into making sure they drinking plenty of water. Sometimes I would begin the lie from the get-go. I'd start off my safety spiel by asserting that while they don't have to necessarily stay together as a group, if they came to a trail junction and the group was spread out, they needed to wait for everyone to catch up. If they found themselves floating somewhere in the middle of the group and didn't see any other people at the trail junction, they were to stop and wait for the tail guide to catch up instead of guessing which route to take. I would then tell them how every year we lose people in the desert wilderness, sometimes for days on end, and that actually we lost two mountain bikers yesterday, so if we come across them we need to make sure to give them food and water, console them, and ... they were swallowing the story hook, line, and sinker.

One of my favorite guides was Jerry. Jerry was amazing. To this day he is still one of my favorite people on the planet. He was a former-marine-turned-CPA who sold it all, moved into the desert, built a teepee, and lived in it. He'd tell stories of getting stung by scorpions in the middle of the night and other anecdotes of living a simplistic lifestyle that belong on reality TV. Jerry also worked as a nature guide and I LOVED getting paired up with him on hikes or mountain bike rides. I could sit and listen to his stories for hours. He also played the Native American wood flute that he would pull out of his pack on breaks. Sometimes we'd be sitting in the shade of a canyon and the songs from Jerry's flute would echo off the canyon walls. Jerry also had the snarky gift of B.S.

As a nature guide he knew everything that moved, crept, crawled, slithered, hopped, or flew. Again, dealing with Manhattanites was fair game for Jerry. Sometimes he'd see another biker or hiker in the distance and Jerry would yell to the group, "Look! There's a hairy-chested nut-scratcher!" But Jerry knew his birds and all of their species and subspecies.

Portland's hipsters are like that ... there are lots of different varieties, species, and subspecies.

It's the same with bicyclists.

Last year I picked up a fun and entertaining book called *Bike Tribes: A Field Guide to North American Cyclists* by bike author extraordinaire Mike Magnuson. He nails it when he writes:

> Nevertheless, for very human reasons, because we don't want to be alone, cyclists tend to gravitate toward other cyclists with whom they feel the highest degree of "alikeness." People who race mountain bikes hang out with other people who race mountain bikes. People who ride bikes for fun hang out with people who ride for fun. It's a matter of group self-selection. Once cyclists become comfortable in their groups, they identify with these groups to the point where they occasionally think things

like *This is the way we do it. That means this is the only way to do it.* Once cyclists think things like that, it becomes harder for them to appreciate that they are part of a larger community consisting of millions of people who ride bikes; instead, they are part of a smaller community consisting of a specific type of cyclist.

Most cyclists typically spend their entire cycling lives functioning within these small units: road riders or mountain bikers or fixie riders or triathletes or cyclocross racers or track racers or people who load their Chihuahua in a basket on a beach cruiser and ride off in the direction of sunshine and music and groovy people who don't want to sweat life's details.

Each of these groups has its own culture and history and a set of rules and normative behaviors. Let's call these groups Bike Tribes. Each of us is part of one tribal group. Each of us is curious about the other Bike Tribes, too, because in that one special way, because we love having two wheels under us, we're all the same.[1]

I have still yet to figure out my own bike tribe. I float in and out of several ones not entirely fitting into any of them. Since I've been riding singlespeeds for years some want to lump me into the urban fixie crowd of hipsters, bike messengers, and wannabes strutting around with their Chrome messenger bags. As I'm now in the over-40 crowd I don't feel like I quite fit that demographic. Besides, I refuse to wear skinny jeans even though I have a couple pairs of Chrome shoes including a city SPD pair that I use when I ride around Portland. But I'm not a roadie. Let me repeat ... I-am-not-a-roadie. Maybe more than skinny jeans I abhor skin-tight

---

[1] Magnuson, *Bike Tribes*, 4-5.

Lycra. Maybe that is the theme I hate, anything skin-tight (except tighty whities). As a result I don't fit into the roadie crowd even though technically I ride a singlespeed road bike. I purposely wear non-roadie cycling clothes, almost as an attempt to introduce mountain bike baggie clothes to the road. I'll get more into fashion in a later chapter but suffice it to say, I get annoyed with all of the roadies with outfits that perfectly match their helmet, sunglasses, bikes, and shoes. Prima donnas, I call them.

I use my bike to commute but I don't feel like a stereotypical Portland bike commuter ... heavy city commuter bikes that have more lights than a 1980s disco and riders wearing more neon than the cast of *Beat Street.* The typical demographic of bike commuters in Portland is what local Portland State professor Jennifer Dill calls M.A.M.I.L.s. (Middle-Aged Men In Lycra). I suppose I certainly fit into that middle-aged demographic but my tap-out is that I don't sport much Lycra so I don't purposely place myself in that category.

OK, I'm being sarcastic about roadies and commuters. I am honestly happy to see people on bikes whether roadies or middle-aged bike commuters or anything in-between. The more the merrier. But what this little detour highlights is that bicyclists are certainly broken down into tribes. I get that, I like that, and I affirm that. To me it makes bicycling more appealing to a larger number of people, while transcending a larger number of socio-economic strata. You see, not everyone has the cabbage to drop $4,500 on a sweet all-carbon road bike or a dreamy higher-end Enduro mountain bike. Those who pick up a crappy fixie on Craigslist for $175 or a low-end bike from Target are in the same category as the Lycra-clad, latte-sipping roadie ... a biker ... a bicyclist ... a person who rides bikes ... in the tribe. This is another reason why cycling is also about equity since it is one of the cheapest forms of transportation.

The fun part about living in Portland is the exposure to the growing variations of bike tribes as the gene pool diversifies. In other cities if you rode a bike it usually meant that you were a mountain biker or a roadie (an obvious exaggeration) but in Portland there is an explosion of all of these different kinds of bike tribes. In a *Darwinianesque* micro-evolutionary way what we find in Portland is a rapidly diversifying number of subspecies of bicyclists which is awesome to behold and to be a part of. The good news is that it is only growing and expanding.

To talk about the different kinds of bicyclists usually means the conversation quickly shifts to different kinds of bikes. So what comes first ... do we gravitate towards bikes that end up defining us, or do the bikes we choose to ride basically explain who we already are to a degree? This is where we fall into the stereotype game which is fun to play, even though it is not the comprehensive tell-all story about people who ride bikes and why they chose certain bikes and bike lifestyles. Again, this is where *Bike Tribes* by Magnuson is a helpful field guide to distinguish the different kinds of riders we see today. With that in mind, and in the same vein, I will instead focus on the bikes more than the riders.

So you're interested in dipping your toes into bicycling in the city. Now what? Where do you start? How do you begin to tackle this intimidating behemoth of bicycling as a mode of transportation and a lifestyle? In some ways it is as a simple as grabbing any old bike, hopping in the saddle, and taking off, but in other more realistic ways it is much more complicated than that. We can certainly argue over the merits of whether it should or shouldn't be complicated, but it is usually a more involved process than we initially realize as it takes at least some minimal investment beyond the bike itself. Depending on where you live it also means buying other essentials such as lights, fenders, packing a pump and spare items (parts, tubes, etc.), and if you're in a city like Portland, rain gear.

So let's say you have a low-end $200 bike. You could potentially be dropping another $200 just for gear to get going. Is this cost prohibitive? Maybe to a slight degree, but given that the average American spends $8,000 a year on their car, $400 is just about nothing. But it isn't nothing. It still costs money to get into it. If you're not in a wet climate you may chuckle at the notion of fenders and rain gear (which can mean rain jacket, rain pants, and shoe covers) but there's nothing worse than showing up for work in soaked blue jeans and underwear not to mention wet shoes and feet. This also means looking into some kind of waterproof bag since the last thing you want is your $250 Chrome Book to get thrashed in the rain or your $1,200 MacBook Pro to get waterlogged. Now you can see why start-up costs can be intimidating or cost prohibitive for many.

When we first moved to Portland I had all of the gear that I needed to ride on a daily basis ... as long as I was mountain biking in arid southern Arizona. No fenders, no rain gear, no waterproof bag, and heck, no road bike. Just a mountain bike with knobby tires and plush suspension forks. I didn't even have a bike lock and the only light I ever used was for mountain bike racing at night. I had to go out and over time begin accumulating all of the essential gear needed in order to bike 365 days a year.

Not everyone can go out and buy every needed item in one fell swoop. I certainly couldn't. I started with a bike ... a cheap singlespeed road bike with a steel frame and crappy components (what little it had). After the first few rains I saw the brilliance of fenders and bought the cheapest ones I could find. Eventually I began rounding out everything else I needed ... lights (front and tail), rain jacket, rain capris, shoe covers, and a waterproof messenger bag. When all was said and done it was a good 18 months from start to finish of acquiring these items. Over time I made a number of upgrades on my bike including crankset, wheelset, handlebars, stem, bottom bracket, saddle, seatpost, etc. Again, it takes time and money.

So, you want to ride in the city? OK, how? What kind of bike do you prefer? The reason I ask this is that this will ultimately begin slotting you into one of Magnuson's bike tribes. In some ways, although we may chafe at this notion, we are defined in part by the bikes we ride. Don't believe me? OK, then let's try this. What is the first image that pops into your mind when I mention the following bikes ... $5,000 carbon road bike, $125 1990s steel frame Diamondback rigid mountain bike, $3,000 custom hand-built commuter bike from a local frame builder, $500 steel frame fixie road bike, $2,500 full-suspension mountain bike, $5,000 cargo bike, or a $25 no-name bike from Goodwill ... Not only do various images come to mind when we think of these bikes but we begin slotting who rides these bikes, why they ride these bikes, and we probably move into conversations about socio-economics.

What this means is that buying a bike is not about simply buying a bike. Often it is about joining a bike tribe. Make no bones about it, bike tribes vary in culture and couth between the sub-species. Just like the dude who buys a $40,000 BMW as a status symbol, many buy bikes as a reflection of status symbols, while for many others a bicycle is their ticket to mobility and job access because they may not be able to afford a car. I'm not trying to pigeon-hole you one way or the other but I want to honestly bring up the reality of these bike tribes as defined by the bikes their members ride.

Yesterday I was out in Hood River (a town an hour east of Portland in the Columbia Gorge) mountain biking for the day. I stopped at my go-to coffee shop (10-Speed Coffee) which is attached to a mountain bike shop (Dirty Fingers Bicycle Repair). As I sat at the table next to the window sipping my coffee I watched the scene unfold inside and outside the bike shop. Since 10-Speed Coffee and Dirty Fingers are attached one can easily slip from one place to the other. That gave me a front row seat to watch all that was taking place in both shops. Since it was a holiday there was a group of grizzled mountain bikers that had assembled to go riding together. With scruffy beards, $3,000 mountain bikes, redneck pick-ups trucks, baggy mismatched clothes with various mountain bike clothing logos plastered across them, one could tell they were serious about their craft. But they also looked like they could be heading out to hunt deer and make moonshine. The point? This is a sub-species of mountain bikers ... free-ride mountain bikers. Crazy lot. Tribes and sub-tribes are everywhere ... and all based on the bikes they ride.

I feel I'm "inter-tribal." I'm stuck between a couple of different tribes while not fully immersed in either. Again, as I mentioned before, I rock a singlespeed road bike, but it isn't a fixie. But I'm not fully "in" because I'm a middle-aged dude with children which separates me a bit from a 24-year-old fixie rider. I love Chrome gear ... shoes, clothes ... and I love the kinds of social media they produce as they promote a strong urban bike culture and value with their brand. But I'm not all in. On the other hand I am a mountain biker but a weird one. I don't care for higher end full-suspension bikes. Instead I opt for a basic singlespeed 26er with front shocks that I built up for under $1,000 (which has changed even during the course of this writing, but more on that later).

For me it is not about needing something high-end in a bike. I remember my first mountain bike race as I was just getting into mountain biking right out of college. I had a crappy fully rigid Diamondback that was barely a step up from a Wal-Mart bike. I didn't have any fancy clothes but I did have clip-in shoes. Showing up at the race was super intimidating as everyone was rocking sweet full suspension bikes with matching Lycra outfits. I had on a cotton t-shirt from my college and cycling shorts underneath some hiking shorts. Yeah, I looked like a dork. I was too embarrassed to warm up and just sat there on the tailgate of my friend's truck. "I am going to get smoked," I fretted as I watched other riders stretch, exchange secret mountain biking handshakes and fist bumps, and look darn cool doing it. I was "that guy" ... you know, who stands out, not in the in-crowd.

The race started and we were off. It was only a 24-miler but I started at the back of the pack with my tail tucked between my legs. But after about the first mile I noticed something … I began passing people. One by one I passed other riders or I'd pass them in packs at a time. On the climbs I ripped up the hills passing even more of them. I soon realized that I had passed most of my competitors, and my confidence grew. I ended up finishing something like 28th out of 250 riders. I was elated. I *could* do this. I also learned that day … it is not about the bike.

Maybe the moral of my own story is that I don't really care to go mainstream and all-in with any particular tribe. Just be myself. I now realize that I am speaking out of both sides of my mouth. On the one hand, I say, be yourself, pick a bike, and just ride it. Who cares what others think? Who cares if you know the in-house language, the secret handshakes, or this notion you have to like all of the subcultural trappings that come with this particular bike and tribe? And yet on the other hand I can't deny that bike tribes are defined by the bikes they ride. These tribes may begin casting you in a certain mold but the good news is that you don't have to play by the rules. Just be aware of them.

And yet again, bike tribes *are* pretty cool. You see, a tribe is like a family, a pack, a herd. You become close to others in the tribe, you ride your bikes together, and you share a common cultural narrative. To be honest, that's not bad. It can even become an awesome experience. During my little excursion to Hood River, I found myself thinking, "Whew, it'd sure be fun to go riding with them." Instead I hammered up and down the hills on my singlespeed hard tail all alone. I need a tribe too. I don't want to communicate that tribes are bad because in actuality there are pretty sweet. In a mobile society they become like family whether they're grizzled mountain bikers or tatted bike messengers on fixies.

With that said, let's continue to have more fun as we look next at a few different kinds of bikes and the various tribes that ride them.

Chapter 6

Redux

If you're looking to jump into urban cycling, one of the first things you'll need to decide is which bike to get. This is your entry point, plain and simple. As I tried to explain in the last chapter, when you snag a bike you're also signing up for a bike tribe. Again, this is pretty cool and part of the fun. Just be mindful of this as you're sorting through which tribal rituals you want to go through in order to join. Each tribe is tied to a bike and as well tied to certain tribal rituals. For some you'll need to buy super-expensive carbon bikes, plus matching skin-tight Lycra, shoes with carbon soles, $200 sunglasses, and a love for high-end wine. For other tribes the required apparel is skin-tight jeans, and instead of sipping thoughtfully on aged wine you're slamming PBRs on your fixie.

For the past nine to ten years I've been exclusively a singlespeed rider whether on a mountain bike ripping around the trails or a road bike in the city. I get asked by a lot by friends who want to pick up a bike for the city and fortunately or unfortunately my default is to always tell them to get a singlespeed. Over time I've learned to temper my enthusiasm knowing that not everyone likes long climbs on a singlespeed up such places as Rocky Butte or Mt. Tabor. Instead, I always ask … *What kind of riding do you want to do? How far will you be riding? Do you want to commute or ride to coffee shops and pubs? Is this going to replace a car? Is this for errands and runs to the grocery store?* Every bike, more so than ever, is built for a purpose.

Despite my love affair with singlespeeds I have come to the conclusion that I need to evolve. It's like when you're watching *Dr. Who* and after a couple of seasons you begin wondering when the Doctor will "upgrade" to his next "version" (we all have our favorites). This past week I made a massive evolutionary leap completely bypassing the missing link. I transformed from a single-cell bacteria straight to an upright-walking *homo sapien*. I jumped from a feathery lightweight singlespeed mountain bike to a full suspension one. It was a technological leap equivalent to going from old rotary phones one day to the latest version of the iPhone, or the leap from a regular screwdriver to Dr. Who's sonic screwdriver in a single day.

In light of this, I am learning to give people better advice when it comes to buying the right kind of bike. One of the online editorials I follow is "The Angry Singlespeeder" at mtbr.com. The premise behind the title is that when you mountain bike on a singlespeed you often *have* to ride angry especially on long sustained climbs where you can't drop easily into a granny gear. It really isn't the most comfortable form of mountain biking and as a result you're bound to be crabby, frustrated when your momentum runs out, and tired from climbing like a bat out of hell. The same applies to city riding ... when you're riding a singlespeed with a tough gear ratio you *have* to ride angry. This past year I literally cracked my steel frame nearly in half from riding my singlespeed loaded down with panniers full of all of the goods I needed for commuting ... extra clothes, computer, food, toiletries, and more layers. This coupled together with Portland's hills meant I put so much torque on my bike that something had to eventually give way ... my frame. For me it was another lesson learned in that not all bikes can do all things. It made me long for a good upright commuter bike with gears and something bigger than 23c rims.

What I hope to do in this chapter is to walk you through the different kinds of bikes to chose from for city riding. There are a lot of choices that can match your needs and lifestyle. Just don't forget the tribal implications for each ...

Commuter Bikes

This is the main staple of urban cycling and includes an enormous range of bikes from low-end to high-end. Technically, anything that rolls and gets you around the city is a commuter bike. Most bike companies now have a line of these ... also called *city bikes, urban bikes*, etc. Sometimes this category spills over into singlespeeds but I'm keeping that category separate for now.

Many commuter bikes look like some sort of cross between a mountain bike and a road bike. Some have flat bars, some come with drop bars, and some have raised bars. There is no uniformity because the key is comfort since you're slogging to work on this bad boy usually either carrying gear on your body or panniers. As a whole these bikes keep the rider in a more comfortable upright position, have a gear range from 3-speed on up, and are usually accompanied with thicker tires than a traditional road bike. These bikes are the bread-and-butter for getting from Point A to Point B in cities.

The freeing element of commuter bikes is that in some ways you don't need to give a rip about what your bike even looks like. It serves a utilitarian purpose … moving your behind (and extras) around the city. The goal isn't to race or be sleek and streamlined, but simply to hop in the saddle with all of the essentials for the work day … extra clothes (if need be), maybe a computer, food, a small dog, bike lock, etc, and get to your job.

These bikes are (or can be) bulkier because of the added weight and the need for them to be durable. Often these are much heavier than typical road bikes even though both bikes share the road. Tires are a little beefier which is a good thing if you're carrying more weight; plus you will want something a bit more rugged if you're dependent upon getting to and from work on this. The fun part of these bikes is that looks really are secondary. If you check out the bicycling scene in cities such as Amsterdam or Copenhagen one of the things you'll notice is the proliferation of nondescript bikes and people wearing normal clothes. Lots of wool and denim and not so much (or very little) Lycra.

From where I'm seated at the coffee shop on this particular morning I immediately see out the window four bikes locked up out front … all of them would be commuter bikes. Fenders, baskets, lights, rack, and a bell round out the essentials. Again, these kinds of bikes are the main staple around here. I have a friend who moved to Portland last year and all that he had was a high-end carbon road bike. *Surely*, he thought, *I already have a bike to zip around in Portland.* Not so fast. After his first ride came the realization that he'd have to lock the bike up against a metal bike staple and run the risk of some hipster with a clunker leaning his bike against his to lock up. After locking his bike up *far* from where he needed to go came the realization ... he needed a sturdy beefy commuter bike. If it gets scratched then, "Oh, well." But what about road bikes? You know, those fancy expensive bikes that skinny dudes who weigh a buck twenty-five zip up and down on through the French Alps during the Tour de France? Next section ...

Road Bikes

Ok, I don't know squat about road bikes ... seriously. In fact, I have a strong aversion towards road bikes and the roadie culture. Yes, that is hypocritical since I ride a singlespeed "road bike." But there's a HUGE difference between cruising around Portland with Chrome City SPD shoes on compared to quintessential roadies with their cute matching outfits, expensive shoes and Type-A personalities. I confess that even though I have an awesome (to me) steel frame singlespeed I do treat it like my "road bike" when not pedaling over to Ristretto or Heart Roasters. Every day over the lunch hour my coffee shop cruiser turns into a vehicle for a good hour to an hour-and-a-half workout. I put on (cough) Lycra and (cough) ride for speed and always try to beat my best time (sans Strava). There's a loop I usually do around the airport and in a typical week I usually log about 100 miles. But I'm not a roadie (cough ... must be something in my throat).

I have a bright white frame with deep-v rims that are blazing white ... you can see me a mile away as I almost glow. I also rock matte black steel fenders. My bike is not light (low-end steel frame and low-end wheelset) but I still get compliments all the time from roadies since I ride a route with a lot of *them* on it. Sometimes they pass me and sometimes (much to their chagrin) I pass them as I'm up out of my saddle pumping hard since I only have one gear and one speed. With all that said, I still don't understand roadies. I'm good with a 25-mile ride on the road (but I *love* 25-milers on my mountain bike) and I wear a mixture of Lycra with cut-off synthetic grandpa dress slacks from Goodwill, and mountain bike jerseys. But hey, in Portland nothing is off limits. But I'd be lying if I said that I understand the roadie culture. If I'm dropping $2,500 on a bike, it is going to be a full-suspension mountain bike with a dropper seatpost and other essentials ... not on a bike that I could lift with my pinky.

OK, I'm getting chaffed thinking about this ... on to the next kind of bike ... singlespeeds and fixies.

Singlespeeds / Fixies

Whew ... where to begin? I could write a book on this topic alone. I must reiterate that I got into riding singlespeeds long before moving to Portland or even owning a singlespeed road bike. The dusty singletrack trails in Arizona were where I first fell in love with singlespeeds and I have been on that trajectory since then ... until last week. While my mountain biking repertoire has expanded I still only have one bike for the city, my singlespeed.

Surprisingly the singlespeed / fixie culture is *not* uniform. There are numerous types of those who jump onto an *uno-speeder*. Mike Magnuson brilliantly dissects the types of riders who hop onto this kind of bike from hipster posers to time trial athletes to bike messengers. He writes that the fixie rider is "a person of mystery to most people in cycling, and because of this, everybody thinks fixies are cool."[1]

So why are singlespeeds so appealing and what makes them a good go-to city bike?

For me, singlespeeds represent a simplicity to riding bikes. They are throwbacks to the days when as a kid your bike only had one speed, coaster brakes, banana seats, and baseball cards wedged into your spokes. That was all we knew. We didn't know of nor fuss about gears. Our bikes were indestructible; it never occurred to us to lube the chain, and over and over we'd beat the crap out of our bikes. When we were done riding we'd slam them down in the front yard as we ran into the house. The bike would sit out in the rain ... the snow ... and bake in the sun. Nonetheless we'd walk out, grab this ticket to childhood freedom, hop into the saddle. and take off. No frills and always reliable.

Singlespeeds or fixies are like that. I tell people the reason why I have a low-end bike is that I can still beat the crap out of it, lock it up all day in the Portland rain while sitting in a coffee shop, get the frame all scratched as it knocks against the bike staples and other bikes, and when I'm ready, simply hop

---

[1] Magnuson, *Bike Tribes*, 185.

in the saddle and go. There are no components to monkey with, replacement parts are cheap, and I don't have to fuss about a carbon frame or a high-end bike with a sweet paint job. My bike is more tank than sports car.

Of course I'm speaking slightly in hyperbole because I do keep the chain lubed and I do clean it ... once in a while. But I don't fret too much about it. As long as the wheels are mostly true, there's plenty of air pressure in the tires, and everything is working decently then I'm content. I don't deny that someday I'd love a nice singlespeed road bike with an aluminum frame, better components and wheelset and such for strictly road riding (not to the coffee shop) for my own personal time trials, but not now.

No bones about it though, singlespeeds and fixies are *urban cool*. I admit that. There is a bohemian / hipster stigma about them and for many who ride them there is an image attached because immediately it places you in the "tribe." As I have done my best to explain thus far, picking the right bike for the city in many ways is more about picking a bike tribe to be apart of and hang out in. Singlespeeds and fixies certainly places one in the younger urban hipster classification and I'm cool with that. I'm sure when a 22-year-old sees me, a 40-year-old, riding a singlespeed they probably assume I'm having a midlife crisis.

But pound for pound and bang for your buck, singlespeeds are the best deal out there. They are a worthy steed to ride. Keep in mind though ... you really only do have *one* speed. If you live in a flat area then you're good to go, but if your city is hilly it can be problematic since most "off the shelf" singlespeeds are geared to make climbing hills not the most enjoyable experience (unless you're weird like me and love hills). However, fret not as an easy swapping of the front chain ring with one that has fewer teeth can put you back on track to more enjoyable city riding. So yes, even though you have one speed there are *a lot* of options out there to making your one-speeder count and be fun for you. But if you're bound and determined to carry a lot of crap around, and not wanting to crack your frame like I did, then maybe you should consider a cargo bike.

Cargo Bikes

Ah yes, the cargo bike. This has been dubbed the "station wagon" of bicycles because not only can you carry a lot of gear, you can even carry all of your kiddos. For the hipster moms out there, this is now urban chic. The advantage of living in a city like Portland is that there is an abundance of all shapes and sizes of cargo bikes. This is not one-size-fits-all. Some cargo bikes have huge front buckets where you can load a month's worth of groceries from Costco while other kinds of cargo bikes look normal but with a rear extension where it is easy to lug around one to two kiddos or gear ... or both.

I have lost track of all of the articles and websites over the past six months talking about the rise of cargo bikes. In many ways, it *is* the new urban station wagon. I live three blocks from a grocery store and last night I zipped over to pick up groceries. By zip I mean drove ... my SUV. Yes, I drove. I walked out of the store with four bags of groceries and a gallon of milk. I'm sure with enough bungee cords and cargo-ties I could've somehow strapped all of this on my singlespeed, but not likely. I suppose I could have made multiple trips carrying a bag or two of groceries at a time. I could have broken my grocery shopping down over several days and picked up little bits here and there and carried it home in my messenger bag. True. But as I walked out of the store pushing the grocery cart to the back of our car I was longing for a cargo bike. Sure, it was raining, but this is Portland so that is a non-factor. But if I had a cargo bike I could have easily put the goods in the front bucket, covered it, and pedaled home faster than it took me to drive. However, I drove. Guilty as charged.

In Portland cargo bikes are used for everything regular vehicles are used for. People move their furniture by bikes rather than renting a U-Haul truck. There's even a great book by Steph Routh explaining it all called *How to Move by Bike*. A lot of local companies do their deliveries via cargo bikes whether it's beer (Hopworks[2]), soup (SoupCycle[3]), or coffee (Trailhead Roasters[4]). And then of course there are the designated urban delivery bicycles (B-Line[5] and Portland Pedal Power[6]). This is just the tip of the iceberg as there are many other small businesses that use cargo bikes to haul plumbing material around and so much more.

I have an old late-80s Diamondback bike that I'm slowly converting into a cargo bike. With such add-ons as the

---

[2] www.hopworksbeer.com.

[3] www.soupcycle.com.

[4] www.trailheadcoffeeroasters.com.

[5] www.b-linepdx.com.

[6] www.portlandpedalpower.com.

Xtracycle FreeRadical[7] anyone can take an existing bike (with a 26-inch wheelset) and convert into a cargo bike. This extends the length of the bike and adds on cargo bags and such. So I'll soon be able to bike to the grocery store and come back with all of my groceries without driving. Can you forgive me now? With that said I now have the bike built up enough with a rack and panniers that I *can* and *do* use it to buy groceries.

I hope my personal story is a consolation. Most of us who love bicycling in the city still have cars. There are very few purists out there ... although there are. I've made as many attempts as I can do go as car-free as I can, but there are limits to what's feasible. We're all in transition and the more we can do on bikes the better we will be physically as well as economically. In addition it gets more cars off the streets and cuts down on pollution and congestion. With the growing proliferation of cargo bikes this gives the average urbanite another tool to be able to continue to expand their errands by bike and use cars less and less. It is an evolution, so take your time, give yourself grace, and have fun in the process.

Anything That Rolls

This past weekend I was in Tucson teaching a seminar on gentrification. One of the sidelights (and highlights) was the various city tours that took place as part of the seminar. The tour that I tagged along on stopped first at Menlo Park on the west side of the freeway out of downtown. This is a new neighborhood surrounded by historic Hispanic barrios

---

[7] www.xtracycle.com.

between the freeway and Sentinel Peak. We stopped at the Mercado San Agustin and a new bike shop that opened only a month ago called Transit Cycles. We met with the owner, Duncan, who shared with us his vision for the shop specifically and bicycling as transportation in Tucson in general. It was an exciting meeting as we stood there amidst a fleet of Soma, Linus, and XtraCycle bikes.

The biggest "a-ha" moment for me on revisiting this city where I cut my teeth in the mountain biking world was noticing how much cycling as transportation has picked up in the five to six years since we left. I was dumbfounded and encouraged of all of the bicyclists I saw zipping around central city neighborhoods, downtown, and the University of Arizona.

My new favorite hangout spot is Exo Coffee just north of the tracks and downtown. With a bike corral out front it was exciting to see many different cyclists come and go as well as zip past. But what was more encouraging and exciting was to see all of the non-hipsters biking. Sure, biking has been a mainstay of transportation among the homeless population, but I saw a lot of people that I could tell relied *solely* on their bicycles as their primary mode of transportation. In fact, for many it was their lifeline to get around this desert city. Which brings me to the importance of this last category of bicycles and bicyclists and that's to simply say that the best kind of bike is simply one that works ... period.

Yes, we can debate, discuss, and do our best to convince others that *our* kinds of bikes are *the* way to go. There's certainly an element of bicycle snobbery involved, but let's be brutally honest here. Who really cares? The most worthy kind of bike is simply *anything that rolls*. When we adopt that mindset it is liberating because it strips bicycling down to its simplest form ... a basic mode of transportation that we *rely on* to get us from Point A to Point B. Every time I see someone riding a crappy Wal-mart bike or a homeless man riding who-knows-what-kind-of-bike laden with plastic bags full of his earthly possessions I am encouraged. As long as it rolls and moves us around, should there ever be any reason to fuss?

Bicycles are great equalizers. Sure, Brazilian fashion models may zip around Williamsburg on a handmade custom bike worth $15,000-$20,000, but at the same time and even on the same street is a homeless man riding a bike he built for free at the local non-profit bicycle co-op so he could move around quickly to pick up cans and bottles to make a living and eat a decent meal. Both riders share the same streets and are enjoying the benefits of bicycling in the city. Obviously there are all kinds of motives as well as all kinds of other factors, but in its purest form, while I may extol the virtues of riding cool singlespeed bikes, at the end of the day I'm simply humbled and grateful that people are out riding. That is the perspective we need to keep before us.

Sean Benesh

Chapter 7

Urban Cycling Fashion and Lugging Gear

Let's get something straight ... I'm NOT a *fashionista*. I
don't claim to be, I don't try to act like I am, and I'll save you
the trouble of Googling my name to see what kind of fashion
plate I am ... because I'm not. I'm a simple dude. I could wear
the same jeans seven days in a row and rotate two shirts and
I'd be content. I get my clothes from thrift stores, Ross or
Target on sale, and that's about the extent of it. I'd rather
spend money on bike parts than another plaid shirt. So why
am I going to dedicate a whole chapter to urban cycling
fashion? Great question. I guess I want to help you think
practically through certain elements of cycling fashion as well
as what essentials to wear while cycling in the city, and because
I do believe I can be ruthlessly practical (and cheap).

With that said, cycling fashion is more important than
you realize. I'm not talking about the latest fashions in
Williamsburg or Wicker Park, but instead about the essentials
to wear to make urban cycling comfortable, practical, and
enjoyable. Unfortunately for many what to wear while
bicycling in the city is one of many obstacles or roadblocks

from using a bicycle everyday as a mode of transportation. On top of that if you add to the mix a wet climate like Portland and the Pacific Northwest then there are literally more layers to the conversation. So you want to bike in the city ... what do you wear?

Believe it or not, but most mornings as I sit in a coffee shop and watch the constant stream of caffeine-deprived Portlanders fuel up for the day I see very little Lycra. In fact, most are wearing ... you know, "just" clothes. Nothing bike-specific, a little bit of synthetic fibers here and there, and lots of wool, denim, and so on. The American mystique about bicycling is that people who ride bikes do so for recreational purposes which entails an uncomfortable relationship with form-fitting and awkwardly-revealing Lycra. Who would want to sit in a coffee like that? Conversely, wherever bicycling is king globally it usually means that a lot of normal looking Joes and Janes are pedaling around the city in clothes they'd wear to work, to the grocery store, to the pub, or on a date. It is really not that complicated.

As I noted in the last chapter, I just got back from a recent trip to Tucson where I had lived for a number of years. Tucson has always been known for its intense bicycling culture with numerous pro road teams training there during the winter months. Sure enough even on my short trip there I saw numerous packs of serious road cyclists decked out in matching Lycra, high-end sunglasses, and golden shaved, muscular legs. They were training hard and riding fast through the city. That is the Tucson I have always known, that and an equally Lycra-clad segment of cross country mountain bikers taking advantage of 300-plus cloudless days a year. But after a six-year absence what I did notice the most was also the most startling.

From the big windows of Exo Coffee I watched as bicyclists streamed by on their way to work, to class, or for errands. But they didn't wear Lycra. They weren't in a hurry. They looked like they were enjoying themselves as they rode through the sun-kissed streets at a leisurely pace. They were wearing "normal" clothes. They were and are simply people who use bikes for transportation. I don't think any would self-identify as a "cyclist." Just a "person" who rides a bike to get around.

We need that kind of normalizing framework when we talk about urban cycling fashion. You see, this really isn't a chapter on the latest trends in urban hip fashion. My big fashion "a-ha" moment is this ... just wear your normal clothes. That's it. This seemingly simple act is one of the best ways out there to encourage more people to bike. If they see that you don't need special clothes or special bikes or anything prohibitive then it lowers the barriers to get more people onto bikes. But what would a chapter on urban cycling fashion be without at least *some* tips and suggestions?

I have picked up a few tricks along the way in terms of urban cycling fashion that I'd like to pass along to you. I'm not Yoda or anything, but I have helped a few people think through different aspects of what to wear while cycling in the city as a lifestyle and mode of transportation. Ready? Here we go ...

There are a lot of traditional cycling clothing lines that have jumped into urban cycling fashion. Whereas they for years have made jersey and padded Lycra shorts they are now delving into creating clothing that is durable, fashionable, water-resistant (or water-proof), and sweat-tolerant. That is good news. The bad news? It'll cost you your first-born child, three cows, two chickens, and a barrel of apples. And we're not talking about bikes because we already have one, right? We went through the process and picked up a sweet ride that we're proud of. But now we have to go out and get city-specific bike-friendly clothes that'll cost half the price of our bike to acquire? Prohibitive.

I found a way to cheat the system.

When you're cycling in the city you have this innate desire to wear clothes that at least have a minimal performance element to them but do not look nor overtly function like a form-fitting Lycra onesie. At the same time you really do want to look "normal" and forgo the adult onesie look that elicits sideways glances at the coffee shop or pub. As I mentioned above, many cycling clothing lines are spitting out urban cycling clothes that have a performance element to them and yet are stylish. You can sit across from someone in a coffee shop and not feel like you're having a dream about standing in the lunch line in junior high in your underwear.

So I thought it'd be prudent to buy some of these new options in urban cycling fashion from my local bike shop. One flip of the tag and finding out the shorts alone cost $100 was all I needed to figure out an alternative. In the land of Portland where DIY is part of the fabric of city living I didn't hesitate to look for a way to cheat the system. I wanted what these new lines of urban cycling clothing have to offer, but at the same time I didn't want to have to take out a loan against my bike to do so. So I went to the thrift store ...

These new clothes extol the virtues of the best performance that normal cycling gear has to offer but with the fashion of urban chic. When I looked at the shorts for example all I saw was shorts like my grandpa used to wear (polyester) and hemmed at the bottom. I rummaged through the thrift store and found several awesome dress slacks that were made of polyester. Probably they were someone's grandpa's dress slacks from the 70s or at least a pair of slacks from Ron Burgundy's wardrobe. But they were legit. With these slacks stuffed in a plastic bag I headed home.

I put them on, figured out where I wanted to cut them into shorts, and did so. Since I can't and don't sew I knew I had to figure out a way to keep the newly cut ends from fraying. So I grabbed a lighter and melted or singed the bottoms of the shorts and *voila!* New urban chic cycling shorts! I think I spent $5 to $6 for the dress slacks that look almost identical to the ones my local bike shop was trying to sell me for $100. I felt like I was in an episode of *Survivorman* except the wilderness I was surviving in was the city. I didn't have to eat bugs to survive, but I could shop at thrift stores to get my fill of urban cycling clothes.

The bottom line of urban cycling fashion is to continue to normalize wearing *regular* clothes (or at least regular *looking* clothes). When more and more people see other people comfortably riding bikes looking like them instead of being garbed in Lycra onesies it'll be more of an encouragement for them to hop in the saddle and try it themselves. Of course anything can be taken to extremes and there are always those who really do want to cough up the dough to buy expensive stuff like you see in *Momentum Magazine*, but that is also OK and even helpful because it elevates the image of people biking in the city.

Sitting here this morning in the coffee shop as I was typing I looked up and took stock of what different people were wearing. Knowing that a lot of people biked over here or were passing through on bikes, the only way I could tell if someone biked here was *not* by what they wore. The give-away was the bike helmet and the waterproof messenger bags. In other words, people riding bikes were wearing the same stuff as everyone else. What I'm saying is there does not and should not have to be a dress code for cycling. Sure, some may wear synthetic materials (many prefer wool) that wick away sweat or dry faster from the rain, but by and large the foundation of urban cycling fashion is this ... just be yourself, be comfortable, and wear normal stuff.

Lugging Gear

For many one of the biggest obstacles of bicycling as a way of life and transportation revolves around hauling stuff ... you know, your computer, extra layers, extra clothes, coffee, groceries, and the like. Everyone has their own preference whether it's a cargo bike, panniers on their commuter bike, a bike trailer, messenger bag, to name a few. The bottom line is, find a system that works with you. The options vary greatly ... but what about you?

For me I've been all over the board in trying to figure out the best way to haul my gear around the city. I've gone from a one-strap sling messenger bag to a full-on backpack messenger bag to panniers and now back to my backpack messenger bag.

I had got to the point where I was carrying so much weight it hurt my back to lug it all around. I felt like I had to be Les Stroud on my bike: ready for anything that came my way. I was ready for a blizzard in mid-June and could peal away layers in mid-February if the sun popped out. But my back would be screaming and writhing in agony by the time I got home, especially on my "hill days."

Finally I switched to panniers and that only made matters worse. It gave me a newfound sense of freedom to cram even more gear onto my bike, more gadgets and technology, even more extra socks, and more. My commutes became a chore. As I mentioned earlier, I ended up putting so much torque on my bike that I cracked the steel frame straight through. But then again ... I was doing all this on a singlespeed with a geared ratio *not* for commuting with extra weight. I began reassessing what I carried and how much I carried. I planned better, was smarter about my selection of gear, and enjoyed my commuters even more.

Nowadays if I can't carry it in my messenger bag I don't bring it. Climate does play a big factor because around here it is important to always think about rain and protective layers. In sunnier climates that is one less thing you need to bother about. What is essential is to think through where you're going, how far, the needs you will have on the way, and what you'll need once you arrive.

A good option is to leave extra gear at work like extra clothes, toiletries, and so on. For many people this is a preferable way to go. Then once you get to work you can shower and change into your work clothes. (Assuming your workplace has a shower.)

There is a rapidly growing market that caters to lugging gear whether for daily work commutes or bicycle travel. Just this morning I walked outside our apartment block and saw parked out front a homemade bicycle contraption that looked like something out of a B-grade sci-fi flick that would be more at home in Area 51 than on the streets of Portland. It was a bicycle, but more like a camper with a bicycle built onto the front. It was all handmade and I'm sure there was an electric assist built in. Talk about not only creatively lugging gear but moving your life's possessions around as well.

With the growing bicycle industry geared towards urban cycling and commuting it is getting easier to lug your stuff around. Sure, you still have to pedal, but with the growth of ebikes and the like it doesn't have to kill you. All of this growth and momentum continues to elevate the appeal and reality of living a bikeable or bike-oriented lifestyle. With every new innovation the obstacles to living this way are falling by the wayside. Also, the greater the growth and the more products available, the more accessible and affordable they become. Even if low-end companies like Wal-mart and Target can carry cheaper versions of Ortlieb or Chrome bags and panniers, it simply means more people can access and afford these products. Sure we may guffaw at the quality of these cheap products and want to push people towards nicer products, but not everyone can drop $160 on a waterproof messenger bag.

OK, that is about all this Bohemian can honestly talk about fashion. Now that we know how to dress and how to carry our stuff around, what about actually riding in the city?

Chapter 8

Rules of Engagement

I'm naturally competitive. Over the years I've learned to temper my enthusiasm and passion because it would often drive me to do stupid things. I've been out on summit attempts (day-hiking, mind you) and I've pushed myself beyond rationality because I was so driven to reach the top. I've ignored the presence of impending thunderstorms to ascend a mountain peak in the desert. I'm not so bright that way, but thankfully over time I've learned to check my zeal and enthusiasm.

That also explains why I've had to begin following about a dozen different college football teams. You see, my Saturdays and weekends would rise and fall on how my team did. I would pace in front of the TV during close games in a cold sweat and practice any superstitious rituals like turning my cap inside out if it meant somehow it'd give my team a competitive advantage and favor with the football gods. But after a while I got tired of the emotional roller coaster ride so I got off it and began following a bunch of teams so regardless of what happens on a Saturday at least some of my teams will win. I know, that sounds weak.

It should be no surprise that my daily bike commutes are for me on par with a crucial mountain stage in the Tour de France. I don't just commute ... I race. I know, I'm *that* guy. Guilty as charged. I emotionally pound my chest when I gobble up riders on my way home and inwardly fume when someone passes me.

The first and only time I've been pulled over by a cop in Portland was actually when I was on my bike. I was out for a training workout ride over the lunch hour. It was lightly raining and I had my gear on pedaling throughout North Portland that day. I'm pretty committed to stopping at all stop signs and stoplights even though many cyclists in Portland refuse to do so. I believe that if we want rights on the road then we need to follow the rules. Little frustrates me more than when I see bicyclist after bicyclist blow stop signs (or stoplights) without hesitation. From time to time I have conversations with non-cyclists in Portland and the most common complaint is their frustration with all of the people they see on bicycles disobeying traffic laws. I nod in agreement.

But on this fateful day I threw caution to the wind when on my workout ride I was passed by a twenty-something in blue jeans riding a fixie. *How dare he?!?!* As soon as he got by me I kicked it into gear ... well, since I ride a singlespeed I don't mean that literally. I stayed on his tail for the next block or so until we came to a busy four-way stop on a semi-busy intersection. I watched in frustration as this hipster dude ahead of me didn't even slow a bit when he came to the stop sign. He blew right through and kept going. Of course my competitive nature kicked in ... I blew the stop sign to keep pace. *I'm not letting him get away.*

However, ten seconds later I caught the site of flashing lights out of the corner of my eye. I turned my head and my heart sank as I saw a motorcycle cop on my rear. I pulled over hoping that he was simply trying to get past me. I sunk even lower when he pulled over with me. *Well, there's no sense in denying the obvious.* When he walked up I already beat him to my traffic violation. Like a schoolboy caught shooting spit wads in school I squealed and confessed my egregious error.

Luckily it was two days before Christmas and after a stern warning he mumbled something about "tis the season for giving" and he let me off the hook. Feeling sullen I pedaled home. I never saw that hipster again. When I got home I told my family. They all laughed hysterically. My competitiveness got the best of me that day.

I still commute with the fury of an angry singlespeeder. You see, for me a commute isn't simply a commute, it is my workout (on the way home). Yes, again, I'm *that* guy. But, I do have to defend myself a little bit here. In Portland you're either pedaling up hill or down, at least where I live. On top of that, since I ride a singlespeed it means I only have one gear ... *haul ass.* When you're climbing you're all in because you can't drop into a granny gear. This means for commuting there's never really time to take the foot off the gas except when descending. With that said, like a shark that goes nuts when he smells blood in the water, when I see another rider up ahead of me it means only one thing ... I'm going to catch him or her (or at least try).

Now that we've pealed back the curtain into the inner recesses of my own troubled psyche, there are certain road rules and what I call "rules of engagement" for living and commuting by bike.

What to Wear

This is not a rehash of the last chapter on urban cycling fashion. But there are certain clothing essentials that make commuting doable and more enjoyable. Also keep in mind that this is a nuanced and contextualized conversation because what is essential to wear for commuting in Portland varies greatly than what you'd wear in Tucson. This weekend I took the train from Portland to Seattle for a graduate level course that I was teaching. Since Amtrak is very bike-friendly I brought my bike along because I needed a way to get around central Seattle. It was an easy trip to plan bike commuting-wise because I had all of the essentials for wet weather commuting.

I have seen several blogs and research results that address how visible bike commuters really are. Usually they are almost glowing with bright neon yellow jackets and helmet covers. But they may not be as visible as they'd like to believe. I'm not trying to rain on your parade, but until we have a whole system of separated cycle tracks away from moving vehicular traffic there will always be risks with bicycling for commuting, errands, and as a way of life. However, the same logic applies to driving cars with tens of thousands of people killed each year in auto wrecks. That doesn't seem to deter people from driving.

Many who bike-commute try their best to be as visible as possible with bright clothes. Since I stopped wearing neon in the 80s simultaneously with forgoing parachute pants, I abhor neon bike gear. Sorry, I have to be honest. I get it, I understand why many do wear it, but I just can't bring myself to do it. Fortunately or unfortunately I love the color black and all of my gear reflects this. My consolation is that my blinking lines and reflective gear will suffice, but it is a risk nonetheless, regardless of what color of gear one wears.

By my second winter of bike-commuting in Portland I went out and bought a new bona fide waterproof bicycling jacket. With pit zips, flaps, reflective stripes, and drawstrings I was ready for near hurricane force winds and rains ... which is not far from reality when the winds come ripping down the Columbia Gorge. By the end of the rainy season I noticed leaks here and there in my jacket and I would end up getting a bit wet on my bike rides. This past year I said, "Forget it," and went to Target and bought a cheap rain jacket. Plus I wanted something a little more stylish ... OK, I know what you're thinking ... "Target" and "stylish" do not go together. Sure, I could've sold a kidney and bought a swank Chrome waterproof jacket, but Target would have to do. And it did. The jacket held up great, it works like a charm, and is almost stylish compared to my previous bike-commuter kind of jacket. Plus it didn't cost me much of anything. Sometimes practicality and budget win out at the end of the day.

I make it my aim to be ruthlessly practical and cheap when I consider what to wear. As I mentioned in the last chapter, I've found my own life hacks of getting maximum performance out of my gear but at the fraction of the cost. You just need to know your climate well and the essential gear you'll need to ride comfortably year-round. For Portland it is always about layers and waterproofing. For cities like Tucson ... fenders? No. Maybe a thong is all you'll need in the eight months of summer. Well, that plus clip-in shoes and loads of sunscreen.

Pack Riding

Bike-commuting is a Darwinian experiment if there ever was one in modern society. It is a strange phenomenon to behold and participate in. It drives me nuts but I've learned to adjust and enjoy some of the benefits from riding in community. I've received fist bumps and high-fives from strangers and have engaged in fun conversations while pedaling next to people I've just met ... all because we have in common riding a bicycle. But apart from that, pack riding reminds of when we had pet piranhas as a kid. It was scary awesome to throw in a piece of lunch meat and watch the feeding frenzy happen. Bike commuting has a bit of the same frenzied ferocity to it. We're trying to get to work, time our speed with the next traffic light, or hope that we don't get stuck on Hawthorne Bridge waiting for the bridge to be lowered so we can cross.

Then there's the natural competitiveness that comes in pack riding. You know, the same things we struggled with in junior high that are only amplified in adulthood. We compare our bike to what others are riding. We also compare clothes and gear. *Doh! That dude has a sweet new Chrome bag. Man, my bag sucks. I need a new bag. $220? Wow, what can I sell on*

Craigslist to afford one? Maybe there's a cheaper one on Craigslist? Argh, the light turned green and I wasn't paying attention and this dude just yelled at me. Why don't people just chill out on the commute? Wait, I don't ...

We compare our bikes with others, our gear and clothes, our helmets, our shoes, etc. Heck, we even compare our fenders, our lighting system, and other little quirky things that are really non-essential. The thing about pack riding is that you want to be at the front of the *peloton* without looking like you want to be at the front. You try your best to mash on the pedals without looking like you're mashing on the pedals. You don't want to be that *race face* guy or gal grimacing, huffing and puffing, and sweating while you pull away ... but you still want to pull away.

So what Jedi-like advice could I pass along about pack riding on your daily commute? Make it fun. That's probably why I go crazy on the way home with pedaling hard. I *need* to make it competitive because it keeps me motivated and looking forward to it. I also vary my routes daily. Some routes are for my "hill days" where the ride intense, and others are my "pedal cadence" days where I ride longer at a steady pace. Also, by varying it I discover new parts of the city to explore while becoming acquainted with more and more bike routes, secret routes and such through the city. I always travel with a bike map so I'm good to go wherever I want to go.

Other Essentials About City Riding

I am going to go out on a limb here and reiterate this ... follow the traffic laws. I know, I know ... that is uncool and makes me sound like a curmudgeon. There are many things we can do to elevate the importance and reality of bicycling for transportation, and one of the key ingredients is that we want people to take us seriously. As long as we're blowing through stop signs and stoplights people who don't ride bikes will continue to build their case against us and the gap widens. It is a reality and a topic lightly tread upon, but Portland's bicycle ridership has been stagnant since 2008. We cannot seem to push beyond the six-percent mark. If sixty percent of the population are in the "Interested But Concerned" category, then watching us riders act irresponsibly only continues to ingrain the maverick nature of urban cyclists.

When I was on my Seattle trip last weekend I came to a four-way red light at a really busy intersection. To my angst I watched as two different riders (one a college dude and the other an older M.A.M.I.L. in his 50s) both disregard the red light and blow through the intersection while I sat there waiting. My first thought (unfortunately) was ... *Well, at least it is not only Portlanders that blow traffic lights.* If this reinforces my curmudgeon persona then so be it, but isn't our goal to get more people on bikes? Sure, a large part of this is certainly better infrastructure including more separated cycle tracks. But we also want to be taken seriously for having chosen bicycles as a viable mode of transportation.

Last summer in the midst of my frustration with all of this I decided to do my own little on-the-fly spur-of-the-moment research into this. I live in a mixed-use building above the entrance to a library at the corner of a busy four-way stop. I walked out on my patio, leaned over the edge, and decided to count the behavior patterns of the next ten cyclists I saw to see if they'd stop at the stop sign. I notice daily the number of riders on this busy bike corridor who disregard the stop sign so I was curious as to the numbers. Sure enough, out of ten riders only two stopped at the stop sign. The others simply blew right through. Young, old, male, female, it didn't matter. I know that I need a larger body of research to draw from, but this little snapshot confirmed what I see on a daily basis.

I admit I like watching those outlaw alley cat road races in Manhattan where riders snag rides holding onto buses, zigging and zagging between cars, riding the wrong direction, blowing through stop lights, and being antagonistic (all the while on fixies), but this does not help our cause. Again, if we want bicycles to be taken seriously as a mode of transportation then one of the great apologetics is that we follow the same rules of the road as motorists, are cordial versus combative, and so on. I don't always see too much of that here in Portland.

The rules of engagement of bike-commuting really are simple ... have fun. If that means ride aggressively and squeeze in a workout doing it then do it, if it means alternating your route to explore the city then have fun at it. But my encouragement is at all times to follow the traffic laws.

Sean Benesh

Awkward Transition

Clank! Pop! Pow!

One of the reasons why I ride singlespeeds is because I have grown to hate derailleurs. There is nothing worse than being out on a ride, whether a speedy commute to work, a trip to meet a friend at the coffee shop, or on a long climb while mountain biking up the Syncline trail in the Columbia Gorge, and then hear those dreaded noises ... Clank! Pop! Pow! The sound of the derailleur in rebellion. With so many moving parts and stretching cables it seems like we're always tinkering with our derailleurs.

A number of year ago I signed up to ride in a thirty-mile mountain bike race in the desert. I had trained hard, sweated profusely, and almost passed out from heat exhaustion and dehydration in preparation for the big day. However, not even five miles into the race, while on a steep climb, my derailleur rebelled, decided to break off, snapping my chain and bending the hanger. In essence I was screwed. Race over. However, it was ten miles to the next checkpoint so I rerouted the chain, bypassed the derailleur, and made it into a singlespeed. I made it to the checkpoint where my family was waiting. I left the race and went out for pizza with them instead.

The chain goes through an awkward transition when the derailleur gets out of whack ... Clank! Pop! Pow! At times it is almost violent in its abruptness. That's what this little interlude is about ... this is this book's awkward transition from where it has been to where it's now going. You've been warned.

Chapter 9

Putting Urban Into Urban Cycling

This is a book on urban cycling, right?

This chapter marks a break or (awkward) transition from where we've been going to where are now. We're taking a turn, the right (or was it left?) fork on the road. Up until this point most of what I've discussed was more or less advice, how-to's, tips, and so on for those jumping into cycling in the city. Which bike is best for you? What kind of rider are you? Which bike tribe will you identify with? How can you lug around your MacBook Air and look cool in the process? But now I'd like to talk to you about the city.

If you happened to flip ahead in the book (if you're *one of those*) you'll see the last chapter is about trying to maintain a balanced perspective on this whole urban conversation (but don't read that chapter yet). It was and is an attempt to juxtapose my love for urban cycling and mountain biking in remote areas, but for now I want to dive into all-things urban.

I love cities. I am passionate about cities. I love large, complex, high-density, diverse cities. The greater their density and energy, the better. In that regard I'm reminded constantly that Portland often feels like a sleepy little town. I say that more with affection than disdain because I enjoy Portland with its bohemian culture and flare, but dense it is not. More and more (as I'll address in the next chapter) you have to leave the central city to see diversity as gentrification has stripped the inner city of its once-vibrant ethnic diversity. However, when I head over to Powell Butte to get a quick mountain bike ride in I am all of a sudden thrust into neighborhoods marked by immigration and multiculturalism ... but that's on the outskirts of Portland proper.

Certain cities leave an indelible mark on us for various reasons. As I look back on the thread of my previous writings and books there are certain cities that pop up in stories and examples because they have become anchor points for me when I write or talk about cities. High density cities? I default to Shanghai, Vancouver, B.C., or Manhattan. Diverse cities? Chicago, Vancouver, B.C., Montréal, Toronto, or LA. Bike-friendly cities? Portland, Montréal, Davis, and so on.

For me, the most enjoyable places to bike are cities that offer are a combination of all of these attributes. While I love pedaling around Tucson I'd love to see more density. For that reason Montréal continues to crop up as a beloved urban context to pedal around in as it has the density (in the city center), bicycle infrastructure, the cultural diversity and funk and vibe that makes the experience awesome. My recent trip to Seattle also reminded me of how much fun it is to ride around there. Maybe a singlespeed wasn't the best option for me with all of the crazy hills, but it really was a fun experience, especially on First Hill around Seattle University.

Cities big and small beckon me to bicycle around and explore. When these cities have bike share programs it makes the experience that much more memorable. While Salt Lake City is not (not *yet*) lauded as bikeable on the level of Portland, Montréal, or the Twin Cities, it is certainly making strides in that direction. Add to the mix the presence of bike share and a light rail line from the airport along with the new streetcar line, and traveling there is a blast because it is easy to get around downtown car-free. But what is it about urban cycling that makes it an adventure for me that rivals such experiences as mountain biking down a pristine sun-kissed singletrack trail on a mountain ridge?

Little for me compares to the exhilaration of mountain biking ... except urban cycling. My favorite routes are through the urban core, weaving in and out of traffic, holding a long stall through a red light, keeping ahead of moving cars, and the ease of free parking. And since I ride a singlespeed I'm always playfully imagining I'm more awesome than I really am since singlespeeds give onlookers the impression you are serious about urban cycling. I mean I am, but I'm not, but I am ...

What is about cities that elicit such love and passion in me? I default to a quote from *Triumph of the City* by Edward Glaeser who I quoted earlier in the book. It is a telling quote and explains much (which I will unpack): "On a planet with vast amounts of space we choose cities."[1] Period. We *choose cities*. In a nation with endless wilderness and pristine forests, canyons, and wide-open prairies, we still choose to live in cities. Here in Oregon most of our state's population resides in

---

[1] Glaeser, *Triumph of the City*, 1.

the Willamette River Valley from Portland down to Eugene. The rest of the state is vast wilderness dotted with a few small towns here and there. But we live in cities.

Why?

In his book *Who's Your City?* economist Richard Florida writes about the three most important questions we can ask or decisions that we will make in life ...

What are you going to do? (job, career)
With whom? (spouse, partner)
Where?

It is the "where" question that *Who's Your City?* is dedicated to answering. Chapter by chapter Florida argues the importance of place when it comes to shaping our lives. He notes that when approaching the first two questions we spend a lot of time digging in, researching, belaboring, considering seriously, and so on. We don't take our career paths lightly. In high school we work with counselors who help set us on a career trajectory, and in college we (hopefully) fine-tune that into a major and a degree and we're off to the races. We take dating seriously and there is an enormous industry in dating websites dedicated to help you make informed decisions ... well, unless you simply opt for the mail-order bride. If we spend an inordinate amount of time wrestling with and answering the first two questions then when it comes to place, why then are we so flippant?

You see, place for most of us will be found in cities. In the U.S. (and Canada) we're considered an "urbanized" country with over 80 percent of our population living in cities. Regardless of where we grow up, the common storyline line and trajectory of our lives finds us moving to cities whether large or small. This has an enormous shaping impact and influence on our lives since the city we choose in many ways molds, hones, and shapes us into its image. I see this all of the time and have been through it on a number of occasions.

Every place where I've lived I find myself adopting local customs, fashion, and colloquialisms. When people move to Portland, especially from more conservative parts of society or the country, over time they find themselves adopting the prevailing worldview, culture, and fashion of Portland. Give someone a year and they'll be a coffee snob, wear skinny jeans, drink hand-crafted beer only, pick up a few more tattoos, become more tolerant, and of course bike all over the place.

Richard Florida's assertion of the importance of place, particularly cities, as a significant shaping influence on our lives cannot be understated. It not only affects our lives but even (gulp) successive generations. This place, the city is the pinnacle of our society. I've read it on a number of occasions but I vividly remembering hearing it from a professor years ago ... "the pinnacle of human ingenuity or innovation is the *city*." It is this setting or backdrop where we bicycle. Again, I'm all into mountain biking ... but my life revolves around the pulsating rhythms of the city. I daily pedal through the streets of Portland whether through inner-city residential neighborhoods or the downtown urban core. This is what truly captivates my imagination.

We're drawn to cities because we like being around people. Utopian visions of living in a cabin in the remote wilderness are just that ... utopian. We *really* don't want to live there. Besides getting bored, because there is only so much firewood to cut, raccoons to trap, and birds to feed, we would end up leading a lonely existence. We need people. In *Who's Your City?* Florida quotes economist Robert Lucas who quips, "What can people be paying Manhattan or downtown Chicago rents for, if not to be around other people?"[2]

Living in the central city of Portland was a decisive move for us for these very reasons. This amassing of creative people in this part of Portland really makes it an incubator for all kinds of innovation whether it's tech companies, the bicycle industry, music, fashion, and more. Economists call this *agglomeration economies* which is in essence the savings and benefits that happen when industries collect together. That is why places like Silicon Valley are hotbeds for new breakthroughs. The density and concentration of brainpower and creativity is staggering.

Last week I took part in an event at Velo Cult put on by the Cog Space which is a new co-workspace / incubator that caters to business start-ups in the bicycle industry. For me and a buddy (Drew) it was a great opportunity to begin networking. In the short span of an hour or so we had a number of business cards in our hands and potential meetings lined up. Agglomeration forces were alive and well at Velo Cult that night as we rubbed shoulders with all kinds of bike-oriented businesses ranging from pedal-powered delivery services to bicycle frame builders to bike tech stuff and more. It was an awesome experience. This highlights the importance of cities, especially as we talk about bicycling.

Cities are incubators of innovations where ideas spread quickly from person to person, block by block, and

---

2 Florida, *Who's Your City?*, 61.

neighborhood by neighborhood. The idea of the Cog Space points out the reality of the impact and effect of bike-oriented agglomeration economies and innovation in cities. As their website communicates, "The COG Space is a concept hybrid of a co-workspace / office and accelerator for small bike businesses in Portland, OR. The mission is to bring together Portland-based industry talent in order to share common resources and services, and harness the collective energy to foster new businesses and/or improve existing businesses all while growing the Portland bike culture."[3]

That's urban innovation and collaboration at its finest. The urban geographic locale is more than simply a zip code or even the built environment around us. There's something magical that happens in cities that you don't find out on the trail. That does not diminish mountain biking or getting outdoors, far from it, but what I'm trying to communicate is that ideas, creativity, and innovations are incubated in cities, all of which *enhances* the bicycling experience whether we're cruising around the city or free-riding on a mountain trail. The genesis is still the city.

To revisit Richard Florida, this is why he places such a premium on the third most important decision that we'll make in life … the *where* question defines us in many ways. Urban cycling does define us in ways that we may or may not be aware of. This is always why when cities develop a reputation for being innovative, tolerant, progressive, and livable they are usually on the receiving end of people, most often this creative class, migrating en masse. This also explains Portland's

---

[3] www.thecogspace.com.

continual meteoric rise as a place where "young people go and retire." Truth be told, we indeed are on the receiving end of a glut of college-educated young adults who want to partake in the cultural experiment called Portland ... to ride bikes, have chickens in the backyard, walk the goat around the block, wear skinny jeans, drink locally roasted coffee and hand-crafted beer, and enjoy a vibrant, walkable, bikeable, accessible urban center.

Oddly enough having a mailing address that says "Portland" gives you instant street cred as soon as you step foot outside of Portland. It could be one of the deciding factors as to why you even bought this book ... it came from Portland, it talks about bicycling in Portland, and is published from an artisanal publishing start-up in Portland. If I wrote this same book in Wichita or Cleveland or Orlando it wouldn't be quite the same. That does not diminish the reality that cities far and wide, large and small, are aggressively putting in bicycle facilities, but there's something about "made in Portland" in the bicycle world that garners more attention.

With that said, and as I mentioned earlier, I am continuously encouraged by what I see when I visit other cities and note how fast other cities are putting in bicycle facilities all the while Portland's bike-commuter numbers have stagnated and we're still enveloped in controversy about putting in a bike share system even though many other cities already have in place. We've lost our beloved status as "America's Bicycle Capital" as other cities woo people out of their cars and onto bikes at a faster rate than we are doing. Not only that but many other cities have bought into separated cycle tracks which make pedaling through the city safer and a more pleasant experience.

So why a book on *urban* cycling? Simply put, it is where most Americans live and where more than half of the global population now lives as well. Bicycling in the city is something we need to continue to talk about in order to move the conversation forward. I follow a number of blogs, websites, writers and such, and it has been utterly amazing watching the explosive growth of the bicycle industry. Again, I'm not talking about roadies in Lycra onesies. I'm talking about bicycle fashion, riding comfortably in the city, and the culture and much more from the likes of *Momentum Magazine* to bike builders like Ascari who focus on the fashion side of the bicycling lifestyle. This is encouraging and should be welcomed as it is another selling point to get people more excited about bicycling in the city.

Car companies have nailed it. I no longer have cable television but once in a while I'll go someplace to watch a game or some TV event. One of the most obvious (to me) reminders of car-saturated society is the proliferation of car commercials. Since I no longer receive a steady diet of these commercials I am always struck by how effective they are. You see, every car commercial is *not* about selling a car, but rather about selling a *lifestyle*. What automakers are attempting to do is woo you into car ownership by selling an image, an experience, a lifestyle. *This* car will make you feel sexy, *that* car is your ticket to wilderness adventure and the mountain man life, *that* truck will improve your masculinity, *this* car will let those around you know that you've reached a certain financial status and success in your career, and *that* car over there will let everyone know you're a sophisticated urbanite. I don't remember the cars or trucks being sold, but I know when I'm being sold a lifestyle and an identity that this supposed purchase will unlock for me. That's pretty effective marketing and we're so bombarded by it that we don't even notice it any longer.

In a capitalist society that is how we roll (no pun intended). Marketing is truly a double-edged sword. On the one hand it can lead people to over-consume and to begin placing their identity in things rather than relationships. But on the other hand if done well marketing can help convince people to buy something they didn't realize they needed ... and we *need* more people on bicycles.

What I love about *Momentum Magazine* or Ascari Bicycles is that they are selling people a lifestyle or identity that is centered around the bicycle. If we can make urban cycling more normative we need to creatively use marketing and other consumer-targeting tools to show people what they are missing. Living a bicycle-oriented life is freeing and fun and fellow Americans more than anyone need help to be wooed out of their cars. Again, I'm not anti-cars, but I believe more Americans would transition to a *car-lite* lifestyle if they saw the benefits of urban cycling as a lifestyle and mode of transportation. Sorry to say, but we need to show people that it is sexy, urbane, sophisticated, and adventurous to do so *alongside* it also being normal, everyday, mundane, pleasant, and for everyone. In other words, hitting every social strata from low-income to affluent. Everyone can ride a bike and share the same streets.

When I write about putting *urban* into urban cycling admittedly I am thinking of all of the benefits of bicycling in the city. Why not get around in the city by bike *and* look good in so doing? Besides, we don't want to arrive wherever we're going, whether to work or a pub, all disheveled. This is where Portland has a unique advantage in that the people bicycling here are synonymous with a hipster or bohemian lifestyle which only elevates the bicycle in the imagination of many. Conversely, we need to normalize and elevate bicycling as a mode of transportation and lifestyle among all different ethnicities and socio-economic levels. Urban cycling can and should be for *all*. But is it? Are every people-group in the city this hip on urban cycling? Let's look next at the *other side* of urban cycling.

Sean Benesh

Chapter 10

Gentrify This!

North Williams is a road that straddles the border between inner North and NE Portland (called Albina). For a good portion of the 20th century this part of Portland was primarily an African-American community. Today gentrification is reshaping the neighborhood on both sides of the road with an influx of middle-class whites and new artisan businesses. Once a stereotypical inner-city neighborhood that local officials considered "blighted," it is now thoroughly stereotypical in its gentrification ... or so it appears. However, there are numerous dynamics at hand in this community that make it far from the stereotypical gentrification process. Namely, with Portland's unique artisan economy and culture mixed in with the city known as "America's Bicycle Capital" there has emerged a dynamic form of gentrification and conflict over something as seemingly benign as ... the bicycle.[1]

---

[1] I have also discussed North Williams in some of my other books. It serves as a good case study of the uncomfortable relationship between bicycles, race, and gentrification.

There is nothing stereotypical about urban decay in America's inner-city neighborhoods that entails racism, economic exclusion, disinvestment, redlining, and numerous other social ills being either forced upon or simply allowed in these neighborhoods. Conversely, there is nothing stereotypical about the gentrification process because there are unique dynamics at hand whether it be Brooklyn, Wicker Park in Chicago, Cincinnati's Over the Rhine neighborhood, or the Downtown Eastside in Vancouver. What makes Portland a unique case study in the dynamics of gentrification is that the flashpoint of controversy in this African-American community revolves around the bicycle. Not only that, but also a road—North Williams Avenue.

The Changing Story of North Williams

North Williams reflects the changing dynamics of gentrification in N/NE Portland. This afternoon finds me along this road at Ristretto. Sitting in this coffee shop for a few hours is a good way to identify who lives in this changing neighborhood. However, if the casual observer were to be transported directly into this coffee shop, whether in the morning during the week or at midday on the weekend, the assumption would be that, based upon the characteristics, attributes, and fashion of the clientele, this is a white and very hip neighborhood. Seeing this demographic streaming in and out all day would lead the casual observer to this seemingly obvious conclusion. However, a different reality exists just outside the doors of the HUB building where Ristretto is located.

Like many who visit Ristretto or the numerous other businesses in the HUB building like Tasty n Sons, Sugar Wheelworks, EaT: An Oyster Bar, or the yoga studio, to name a few, I arrive by bicycle. With ample bicycle parking in the form of bike corrals on the street or covered bike parking under the patio, this building is certainly a hub for bicycle enthusiasts. However, the businesses in this building are only part of all of the other surrounding businesses that cater to bicycling hipsters in the area. Across the street from the HUB building is a new location for Portland's beloved Kenny & Zuke's Deli, Hopworks Bike Bar, and even the Portland location for the United Bicycle Institute which offers classes, training and certification for bicycle mechanics and frame builders. Again, to the casual observer, based upon the business types that cater to a particular socio-economic grouping, the presence of predominantly white customers, whether drinking coffee, partaking in yoga, or at one of the eateries, would lead one to suspect that this is a white hipster neighborhood.

But to walk out of Ristretto in any direction reveals a different reality. Across from the HUB building is also Life Change Christian Center, a predominantly black church that was started in the 1950s. Journeying away from North Williams Avenue and into the neighborhood a different picture and reality of life in inner North and NE Portland begins to emerge. The north side of the HUB building, where I park my bicycle at the bike corral. is across from the homes of several African-American families. The further one walks or bikes away from North Williams the more apparent it becomes that this neighborhood is not as white and as hipster as the patrons of Ristretto would suggest. A few blocks further along are several other historic African-American churches and North Portland Bible College, a school that was started in the 1980s to train pastors and members of the numerous black churches in this part of the city.

This is a neighborhood in significant transition. The scene along North Williams reflects the changes taking place in this part of the city. The neighborhood in fact has gone through several in- and out-migrations of people of different ethnicities. My frequent bicycle rides through the neighborhood have made me an eyewitness to these changes. Many of the church buildings that house African-American congregations display the historic transitions taking place. A look at the cornerstones of these church buildings reveals that many of them were started and built by European immigrants, including Dutch and German, a century ago. However, as the 20th century progressed, the neighborhoods around North Williams changed.

Gibson states, "Although the population [of the neighborhood] is very small (never comprising more than 7 percent of the city and 1 percent of the state), Portland provides an interesting case study of a Black community that found itself suddenly in the path of urban redevelopment for 'higher and better use' after years of disinvestment."[2] This is a significant insight because while there are commonalities between disinvestment and forced ghettos and the gentrification that ensues decades later, what makes Portland unique is partly due to its relatively small African-American population. However, the same forces behind segregation that

---

[2] Gibson, "Bleeding Albina," 3.

impacted Portland were the same in other cities with a more notable African-American presence in terms of size. "While the scale of segregation has been very small relative to large cities in the Midwest and Northeast, the consequences for residents are similar."[3] By the 1940s half of Portland's black community was confined to the North Williams Avenue corridor.

While there were forces of homophily—that is, a "love of the same"—at play in the geographic settlement for not only the African-American community but other ethnicities as well, to the degree that many cities have or had a "Little Italy" or a "German Town" or a "China Town," the difference is that for the black community it was most often forced. This forced segregation took numerous shapes and forms. In other words, the forces that created these pockets of disinvestment and decay, whether in housing stock or a languishing local economy, were and are the same forces at work in gentrification. Unfortunately, as the layers that make up the process of gentrification are peeled back, there emerges the fulcrum of race and poverty struggles in urban America.

If only viewed on a superficial level, gentrification as the process of the middle class (i.e., white-collar, creative class) moving back into central city neighborhoods such as along North Williams, there would be no cause for alarm. However, the movement of middle-class whites reinvesting in central city neighborhoods brings other collateral effects such as the displacement of low-income renters and a loss of identity and community for longtime residents. This seems to be the

---

[3] Ibid., 4.

epicenter of the controversy over gentrification in that there are multiple actors and moving parts feeding into these transitions both before and during gentrification. So how did we get there?

Using Brooklyn as an example, Sharon Zukin comments, "For most of the twentieth century Brooklyn had a sorry reputation as a place where artists and writers were born but were eager to escape from."[4] Cities and neighborhoods like Brooklyn, North Portland, or North Omaha are at the center of the gentrification debates. Many of these cities and neighborhoods were once places where people sought to get away from when these areas bottomed-out economically and housing was devalued. Brooklyn serves as a microcosm of gentrification in regards to race issues. The neighborhood has gone through wave after wave of change and transformation, but yet it was and is not uniform nor comprehensive. As *Atlantic Cities* (or now *CityLab*) writer Sarah Goodyear observes, "Depending on who you talk to, the borough of Brooklyn is a great urban success story, a painful hipster cliché, or a provincial backwater. It's actually all of those things, and many more. Brooklyn is a huge place, 71 square miles encompassing old-school blue-collar neighborhoods like Bay Ridge, trendy enclaves like Williamsburg, and decidedly ungentrified sections like East New York, which has some of the highest crime rates in all of New York City. Some 2.5 million people live in Brooklyn, and they are anything but

---

[4] Zukin, *Naked City,* 39.

homogenous."[5] Cycles of health, decay, blight, renewal, and gentrification are not happening uniformly even in places like Brooklyn.

The question that needs to be asked and addressed is, why or how did these neighborhoods become primarily low-income decaying ethnic neighborhoods in the first place? How did these neighborhoods, like inner North / NE Portland, transition from blue-collar Norwegian or German neighborhoods to mostly lower income African-American communities? William Flanagan begins uncovering the layers of race and gentrification, "The population movement that has had the greatest impact on residential segregation in the second half of the twentieth century has been the suburbanization of the white metropolitan population. It produced a pattern in which African American and other minority populations were concentrated in inner cities ringed by largely white, middle-class suburbs."[6] This is reflective of the storyline in Albina, but why did this movement and population reshuffling begin in the first place? How much of population dispersal was and is race-related? As we will see, there are multiple factors for residential clustering for varying ethnicities; some of it is normative and "natural," but in other cases, especially for the plight of African-Americans, the process was more about containment and control by outsiders.

Jeb Brugmann succinctly addresses the plight of African-Americans in the mid-1900s. "Battle by battle, the aspirations

---

[5] Goodyear, "The Trendification of Brooklyn and the Perils of a Successful Urban Brand."

[6] Flanagan, *Urban Sociology*, 291.

that black migrants brought to the city were impeded and steered into their own ghetto-cities. By the 1950s these cities had matured into worlds of their own, creating a parallel urban universe and quietly seeding one of the first urban revolutions of the twentieth century."[7] Because of race, the black community was at a disadvantage as political bosses, business interests, urban planners, and at times the local police, fought black progress.[8] As a result these mostly black inner cities (South Bronx, Chicago's "Black Belt," Inner N/NE Portland, etc.) were neglected and disinvested in which, after bottoming-out, created the ripe conditions for reinvestment and the resultant gentrification process. Through purposeful neglect, redlining, economic and social exclusion these neighborhoods were simply left to free fall. Harvard sociologist William Julius Wilson contends that, "There is no doubt that the disproportionate concentration of poverty among African-Americans is one of the legacies of racial segregation."[9]

Racial segregation and limited economic access and opportunities created despair among the people of these blighted and neglected neighborhoods. The result was the proliferation of an "informal economy" which only made conditions worse. This led to such economic activities as the drug trade and prostitution. "Neighborhoods plagued by high levels of joblessness, insufficient economic opportunities, and

---

[7] Brugmann, *Welcome to the Urban Revolution*, 63.

[8] Ibid., 64.

[9] Wilson, "From Institutional to Jobless Ghettos," 123.

high residential mobility are unable to control the volatile drug market and the violent crimes related to it."[10]

It is easy for outsiders to be dismissive of drugs and crimes in inner-city neighborhoods by laying the blame solely on the residents. This is what Flanagan gets at when he writes about the "culture of poverty" in that poverty, crime, and other such things is a way of life—that in some ways it is a conscious choice of the people in these ghettos. But is it really a choice? Were there other factors involved?

Another way to look at it is to address the "structure of poverty" where economic forces and racism were the catalytic drivers that created and accelerated poverty. This is what Hal Joseph Recinos alludes to, "The violence and drugs in the city are, in part, byproducts of the structures of racism. Powerful leaders of white society have limited the structure of opportunity for people of color, forcing the people of the barrio and ghetto to find other ways to survive. For many, the drug economy provides one form of survival—perhaps for a while—in its violent world of death."[11]

If Flanagan and Recinos are correct, then this reveals a darker side behind the poverty, place and gentrification that is at work along North Williams. People in impoverished neighborhoods were (and are) not just simply choosing this lifestyle; instead the "structure of poverty" has restrained and constrained them, leaving them with limited options to do otherwise.

---

[10] Ibid., 124.

[11] Recinos, "Racism and Drugs in the City," 98.

The root of the problem was and is racism. Racism is more than simply disliking people of different ethnicities. In fact it can create a whole litany of social ills that affect millions of lives. As Recinos boldly asserts, "A walk down any inner-city street tells the story of the results of the international drug business: hopelessness, hunger, economic marginalization, racism, and xenophobia haunt the inner cities of North America."[12] Because of their ethnicity, the African-American populace in the inner cities were systematically and permanently excluded from the market economy which in turn diminished their share of the economic benefits. In other words, not only were blacks spatially segregated by cultural pressures and economic limitations, they were also more or less cut off from access to the market economy. Wilson "argues that the changed structure of the U.S. economy is more responsible for the plight of poor Blacks today than is racism."[13] But is that changed structure a form of racism? Yes.

For most ethnicities and cultural groupings there is the reality of homophily, mentioned earlier. This "desire to be with those who are similar to us is a consistent finding in studies of residential preferences. When choosing housing, individuals more often prefer potential neighbours who share a common racial or ethnic background or recent immigrant perspective."[14] This explains some of the reasons why people, particularly new immigrants, locate where they do in cities.

---

[12] Ibid., 101.

[13] LeGates and Stout, *The City Reader*, 117.

[14] Hiller, *Urban Canada*, 286.

Looking across the urban landscapes of America we can easily point out Italian neighborhoods, German neighborhoods, Puerto Rican neighborhoods, Polish neighborhoods, and so on. The point of differentiation with African-Americans is that not only were blacks often coerced into such collections, but outside pressures, policies and limitations prevented them from ever leaving. As a result, neighborhood after neighborhood which housed African-Americans continued to spiral downward through disinvestment and neglect. "Confronted with high costs and institutionalized neglect, the black districts deteriorated over a mater of decades. Their city was never upgraded or renewed, and its asset value declined, creating a structural impoverishment that still dogs American society."[15]

"In 1959, less than one-third of the poverty population in the United States lived in metropolitan central cities. By 1991, the central cities included close to half of the nation's poor. Many of the most rapid increases in concentrated poverty have occurred in African-American neighborhoods."[16] Ironically, though, these very blighted neighborhoods were soon to become the envy of outsiders and began to entice middle-class whites. In the 1970s "small pockets of the old inner city showed signs of reversal: in some places, government-driven urban renewal programs had created new offices, malls, or upscale residential developments for middle-class, mostly

---

[15] *Welcome to the Urban Revolution*, 63.

[16] "From Institutional to Jobless Ghettos," 121.

white households."[17] These same neighborhoods that had undergone reduced policing, redlining by the banks, and economic disinvestment, now all of a sudden had new capital flowing back in to create a better environment for middle-class whites. Simultaneous to this, and a driver for some of this change, was an evolving lifestyle preference among the middle class which also began influencing locational preferences.[18]

So what we have now are inner-city neighborhoods like what we find along North Williams that have gone through decades of neglect and abandonment. Culturally and economically cut off, the spiral continued downward in both the culture and structure of poverty. Internal and external forces were exerted on these neighborhoods which only exasperated these conditions. While for many, notions of urban renaissance and revitalization projects are welcomed and appreciated, they fail to see the forces that lie beneath the surface. "The sunny view of 'revitalization' and 'renaissance' ignored the harsh realities of poverty, displacement, and chronic shortages of affordable housing."[19]

I recall a recent conversation with a friend who has lived in North Portland for the past forty years. As an African-American woman, she certainly admits enjoying the positive elements that gentrification is bringing to her neighborhood, especially the reinvigorated economic outlook. But at the same time, she says, this does not cancel out some of the dubious

---

[17] Lees et al, *Gentrification*, 43.

[18] Ibid.

[19] Ibid., 44.

policies and practices that allowed this same neighborhood to decline to the point that it did in the first place.

So who is moving into North Williams? And how does this conversation connect with urban cycling?

Sean Benesh

Chapter 11

Bicycles as Vehicles of Empowerment or Exclusion

The flashpoint for the gentrification conversation along North Williams revolves around the bicycle. The cultural appetite for what the creative class likes and enjoys is in stark contrast to that of the African-American community. "North Williams Avenue wasn't hip back in the late 1970s. There was no Tasty n Sons. No Ristretto Roasters. No 5th Quadrant. Back then, it was the heart of the African American community. It was wonderfully colorful and gritty."[1] As the black community saw their own businesses close down through economic disinvestment, they weren't replaced with new businesses that they regarded as desirable. In the several hours I spent today at Ristretto I have seen roughly a hundred patrons come in and go out, plus others sitting outside on the patios of one of several nearby restaurants. Only three were African-American. As I mentioned earlier, the buildings that surround this coffee shop are home to many African-American families. And yet these new businesses do not appeal to their cultural tastes.

---

[1] Smith, "This isn't the North Williams Avenue I remember."

This all came to a head over a road project to reconfigure North Williams and Vancouver Avenue. Both are one-way roads a block apart that carry a high volume of bicycle traffic. Vancouver's southbound traffic flows carry cyclists towards the Lloyd Center and downtown Portland and so sees its heaviest usage in the mornings. Williams on the other hand carries northbound traffic away from the city center which means its highest use is in the afternoons and evenings when bicycle commuters are heading away from the city center. But the focal point of all of this controversy is specifically tied to North Williams Avenue because this is where most of the new businesses are coming in.

A *New York Times* article featured this stretch of road including one of the business owners who opened up the beloved Hopworks BikeBar. "North Williams Avenue [is] one of the most-used commuter cycling corridors in a city already mad for all things two-wheeled. Some 3,000 riders a day pass by Mr. Ettinger's new brewpub, which he calls the Hopworks BikeBar. It has racks for 75 bicycles and free locks, to-go entrees that fit in bicycle water bottle cages, and dozens of handmade bicycle frames suspended over the bar areas. Portland is nationally recognized as a leader in the movement to create bicycle-friendly cities."[2] Other national newspapers and magazines have also picked up on all of the buzz happening along North Williams. In *Via Magazine*, Liz Crain writes, "With 3,000 commuters pedaling it every day, North Williams Avenue is Portland's premier bike corridor. Visitors, too, find plenty worth braking for on two blocks of this

---

[2] Baker, "Developers Cater to Two-Wheeled Traffic in Portland, Ore."

arterial, including two James Beard Award–nominated chef-owned restaurants and a slew of hip shops and cafés."³ *Sunset Magazine* has several features on North Williams including "Go green on Portland's North Williams Avenue: Enjoy a low-key urban vibe thanks to yoga studios, indie shops, and cafes."⁴

With images of happy (white) hipsters pedaling bicycles, doing yoga, and eating gourmet food, the nation is given a taste of inner N/NE Portland that is not reflective of the reality of the neighborhood nor the tension surrounding gentrification. These magazines showcase things to see, do, and eat along North Williams with helpful hints like, "Scene: A low-key urban vibe, courtesy of yoga studios and green indie shops and cafes ... Dress code: waterproof jacket and jeans with right leg rolled up ... Native chic: A waterproof Lemolo bike bag ... The Waypost: Creative types come to this coffeehouse for locally produced wine and beer, as well as live music, lectures, and classic-movie screenings."⁵

However, not all of the residents are necessarily in favor of these changes taking place. And there are certainly other national media outlets who have picked up on the "other side" of the North Williams story. "Located in a historic African-American community, the North Williams businesses are almost exclusively white-owned, and many residents see

---

³ Crain, "Portland's North Williams Avenue."

⁴ Manning, "Go Green on Portland's North Williams."

⁵ Ibid.

bicycles as a symbol of the gentrification taking place in the neighborhood."[6]

The tensions of racism and gentrification have culminated in ongoing debates over North Williams' status as a major bicycle thoroughfare. Sarah Goodyear of *The Atlantic Cities* (*CityLab*) writes, "Sharon Maxwell-Hendricks, a black business owner who grew up in the neighborhood, has been one of the most vocal opponents to the city's plan for a wider, protected bike lane. She can't help but feel that the city seems only to care about traffic safety now that white people are living in the area. 'We as human beings deserved to have the same right to safer streets years ago,' she says. 'Why wasn't there any concern about people living here then?'"[7] This picks us on the tension surrounding the North Williams project in general, and in particular the controversy surrounding repainting the traffic lanes to incorporate new designs which cater to the growing number of bicyclists who use this corridor.

Goodyear goes on to lay out both sides of the controversy:

> Jonathan Maus, who runs the *Bike Portland* blog and has reported extensively on the North Williams controversy, thinks the city should have stood its ground and gone forward with the project, but wasn't willing to do so in part because of the political weakness of scandal-plagued Mayor Sam Adams, who has been a strong biking advocate and is closely identified with the biking community.

---

[6] "Developers Cater to Two-Wheeled Traffic in Portland, Ore."

[7] Goodyear, "Bike Lane Backlash, Even in Portland."

"There's been too much emphasis on consensus," said Maus. "I'm all for public process, but I also want the smartest transportation engineers in the country on bicycling to have their ideas prevail."

Maus, who is white, says the history of North Williams shouldn't be dictating current policy, and that safety issues for the many people who bike on the street are urgent. "At some point as a city, you have to start planning to serve the existing population," he said. "The remaining black community is holding traffic justice hostage. It's allowing injustice in the present because of injustice in the past."[8]

In light of this, why is North Williams the flashpoint for controversy? The tension and angst is about more than simply repainting a roadway; it embodies the most visual representation of gentrification in inner N/NE Portland. For longtime African-American residents, as expressed above by Maxwell-Hendricks, she and others felt that they had simply been neglected for decades. This negligence took the form of economics, housing, and general concerns of safety. Their frustration is that it wasn't until middle-class whites began moving into the neighborhood that these issues began to be addressed and rectified. This notion of systemic racism helped created this area and these same forces are at play in gentrifying this once predominantly black neighborhood.

The African-American community feels it has been slighted once again. The initial citizen advisory committee revealed the imbalance: "Despite North Williams running through a historically African American neighborhood, the citizen advisory committee formed for the project included 18

---

[8] Ibid.

white members and only 4 non-white members."[9] This is why the push for safety along the North Williams corridor has caused such an uproar. "The current debate about North Williams Avenue—once the heart of Albina's business district—is only the latest chapter in a long story of development and redevelopment."[10]

For many in the African-American community the current debate over bike lanes along North Williams is simply one more example in a long line of injustices that have been forced upon their neighborhood. Beginning in 1956, 450 African-American homes and business were torn down to make way for the Memorial Coliseum. "It was also the year federal officials approved highway construction funds that would pave Interstates 5 and 99 right through hundreds of homes and storefronts, destroying more than 1,100 housing units in South Albina."[11] Then came the clearance of even more houses to make way for Emanuel Hospital. For more than 60 years, racism has been imbedded in the storyline of what has taken place along North Williams.

For many, the North Williams project is more than repainting lines. As Maus reported, "A meeting last night that was meant to discuss a new outreach campaign on N. Williams Avenue turned into a raw and emotional exchange between community members and project staff about racism

---

[9] City Club of Portland, "Case Study."

[10] Loving, "Portland Gentrification."

[11] Ibid.

and gentrification."[12] In his article, Maus noted the painful history of Albina as the primary catalyst for the tension today.

> Lower Albina—the area of Portland just north and across the river from downtown through—was a thriving African-American community in the 1950s. Williams Avenue was at the heart of booming jazz clubs and home to a thriving black middle class. But history has not been kind to this area and through decades of institutional racism (through unfair development and lending practices), combined with the forces of gentrification, have led to a dramatic shift in the demographics of the neighborhood. The history of the neighborhood surrounding Williams now looms large over this project.[13]

It was at this meeting that a comment from one of those in attendance changed the entire trajectory of the evening as the conversation quickly moved away from the proposed agenda. One woman said, "We have an issue of racism and of the history of this neighborhood. I think if we're trying to skirt around that we're not going to get very far. We really need to address some of the underlying, systemic issues that have happened over last 60 years. I've seen it happen from a front row seat in this neighborhood. It's going to be very difficult to move forward and do a plan that suits all of these stakeholders until we address the history that has happened. Until we

---

[12] Maus, "Meeting on Williams project turns into discussion of race, gentrification."

[13] Ibid.

address that history and ... the cultural differences we have in terms of respect, we are not going to move very far."[14]

The crux of the conflict is not about bicycles nor bike lanes nor even new businesses and amenities. It is about racism. The push for creating a more bikeable and bike-friendly commuter corridor has raised the ire of longstanding residents who had felt neglected and voiceless for decades. "The North Williams case study is an example of the City inadequately identifying, engaging and communicating with stakeholders."[15]

Now that more whites are moving in are changes taking place. "Some question why the city now has $370,000 to pour into a project they say favors the bike community while residents for decades asked for resources to improve safety in those same neighborhoods. To the community, the conversation has polarized the issue: white bicyclists versus the black community."[16] But is this issue completely race-related? Portland has been and continues to expand its bicycle infrastructure throughout the city, not just in N/NE Portland. There are also several other main bicycle corridors that receive a high volume of bicycle commuters, but since they do not go through any ethnic neighborhoods they have not created this much controversy. This does not minimize the tension and angst over the North Williams project; nor does it downplay

---

[14] Ibid.

[15] "Case Study."

[16] Navas, "North Williams traffic safety plan gives neighbors a chance to delve into deeper issues of race, gentrification."

the role that racism has played throughout the history of that community.

Minorities and Cycling

One of the questions that this case study reveals is the (supposed) connection between bicycles and racism. Are the use of bicycles really about ethnic identity and the preferred mode of urban transportation for a growing number of ethnic whites in central cities? Or is bicycling growing across the board among other ethnicities? John Greenfield, in an article entitled "Bike facilities don't have to be 'the white lanes of gentrification'" writes, "Bicycling doesn't discriminate. It's good for people of all ethnicities and income levels because it's a cheap, convenient, healthy way to get around, and a positive activity for youth and families. So it's a shame that cycling, especially for transportation, is often seen as something that only privileged white people would want to do. And it's unfortunate when proposals to add bike facilities in low-income communities of color, which would be beneficial to the people who live there, are viewed as something forced on the community by outsiders."[17]

In his article, Greenfield explores a similar project in the Humboldt Park neighborhood Chicago. Like Portland, "People in Humboldt Park, a largely low-income Latino and African-American community on Chicago's West Side, once

---

[17] Greenfield, "Bike facilities don't have to be "the white lanes of gentrification."

opposed bike facilities as well."[18] That was ten years ago. Since then attitudes towards bike lanes have changed. Over the last decade there have been concerted efforts to educate people, including children, about the benefits of bicycling as well as related safety issues. The tide has turned, bike lanes have been installed, and the neighborhood has embraced them. In this case the city waited until the community eventually moved from resistance to acceptance to enthusiasm about a bicycle infrastructure before bike lanes were put in.

Again, this seems to be one of the points of tension in Albina because bike lanes were installed long before there was an enthusiastic acceptance by the community. In essence, they felt that bike lanes were simply another in a long line of changes that had been implemented without their consent. It appears that the City of Chicago did it right by taking their time. What it also reveals is the changing attitude among different ethnicities towards bikes and a bicycle infrastructure.

Not too long ago a report was released from the League of American Bicyclists and the Sierra Club called "The New Majority: Pedaling Towards Equity." Sarah Goodyear, in an article for *The Atlantic Cities* (*CityLab*) highlights some of the findings from the report:

- Between 2001 and 2009, the fastest growth rate in bicycling was among the Hispanic, African American, and Asian American populations. Combined, those three groups went from making 16 percent of the nation's bike trips to 23 percent.
- Between 2001 and 2009, the growth in percent of all trips taken by bike was 100 percent among African

---

[18] Ibid.

Americans; 80 percent among Asians; 50 percent among Hispanics; and 22 percent among whites.
- Eighty-six percent of people of color surveyed said they had a positive view of bicyclists. (For the purposes of the survey, "people of color" includes African American, Hispanic, Asian, Native American and mixed race.)
- Seventy-one percent of people of color surveyed said that safer cycling would make their community better.[19]

What this article and this report reveal is the changing attitudes towards cycling among the American populace. This also dispels the notion that bicycling is strictly a "white" thing. Tanya Snyder writes, "Let's get one thing clear: People of color ride bikes. They commute to work on bikes. They ride for pleasure. It saves them money and time, and it keeps them healthy."[20]

In her article, Snyder highlights the tension of bicycling and racism. "'Nobody is against safer streets in their neighborhood,' said Hamzat Sani, equity and outreach fellow at the League of American Bicyclists. 'Cycling organizations just haven't done a good job communicating the message that streets that are safer for cyclists are safer for everyone.'"[21] In some ways this reveals part of the tension involved in the North Williams project. No one is against safer streets. The crux of the angst is that the black community had been marginalized for so long that they felt they had lost their

---

[19] Goodyear, "The Surprising Diversity of the America Cycling Community."

[20] Snyder, "Cyclists of Color."

[21] Ibid.

voice. This came to a head over the proposed bike lane changes because for them, it was more than white stripes on the road, it symbolized decades of marginalization and neglect.

But as this study points out, bicycling ridership is on the rise among all ethnicities. Not only that, but it is growing the *fastest* among the African-American community. The challenge is that, "Unfortunately, communities of color often lack for safe infrastructure. 'Data gathered by the Los Angeles County Bicycle Coalition revealed that neighborhoods with the highest percentage of people of color had a lower distribution of bicycling facilities,' the report says, 'and areas with the lowest median household income ($22,656 annually) were also the areas with the highest number of bicycle and pedestrian crashes.'"[22]

Conclusion

This case study reveals that there are multiple processes and actors involved in the gentrification process along North Williams Avenue. There are macro (global) and micro (local) forces at hand reshaping not only this part of Portland, but also inner-city neighborhood across the country in light of changing economies and cultural preferences as reflected in the rise of the creative class / artisans (and bohemians as discussed in Chapter 1). The clash over bicycles appears to be at its core a sense of continued displacement symptomatic of the long history of racial exclusion. As a new report entitled, "The New Majority: Pedaling Towards Equity," noted, the African-

---

[22] Ibid.

American community is not against bicycles. In fact they represent the fastest growing ethnicity in terms of new bicyclists, even at a faster rate than ethnic whites. The problem is not with bicycles or new bike lanes, but instead the systemic racism and injustice that have for so long oppressed the black community.

This example of what is taking place on North Williams and its inclusion in this book is the equivalent of the "backdoor cut" in basketball. You picked up this book possibly thinking of how to bolster your urban hipster lifestyle and couth, and I am certainly hopeful I have been a help in that direction. However, we cannot talk about urban cycling without noting the larger storyline of how the word *urban* has been used and defined. My desire is to see more people in the city, black or white, use bicycles as a mode of transportation and a lifestyle. The health and cost benefits are simply too staggering to be dismissive. This is where the conversation about bicycling turns to an equity conversation.

Sean Benesh

Chapter 12

Equity and Bicycling

I know what it is like to be dependent on public transit as my only mode of transportation. As I mentioned previously, when we lived for a couple of years in Vancouver, British Columbia, we were car-less for about eighteen months. Now before you applaud my efforts to go car-free and make a bold stand on sustainable transportation, know that the decision was kind of thrust onto us. While I was truly thinking about what a car-free or a car-lite lifestyle would entail, especially with a family of five, our one and only car died.

Normally that would not be a complete show-stopper as we could have scraped the cabbage together to fix it up. But it happened the week that our U.S. auto insurance was expiring and I was about to get new provincial insurance. We were to drive our car to get inspected before we could get insurance and now all of a sudden our car was dead and we were faced with a significant part that needed to be replaced. And so I missed our window of opportunity. We quickly had to jump into the deep end of the pool and figure out how to transition from the only lifestyle we knew (auto-dependent) to being completely transit-dependent.

I'm not a conspiracy theorist when it comes to mobility even though I advocate for more people on bikes and public transit. But having grown up in small-town Iowa meant that the only way to get around was by car. Sure, before the magical age of sixteen I got around fine on a bicycle or my Puch moped (before it was hipster), but life still revolved around the auto. The town's built environment dictated as much since it was built with the auto in mind. Nearly every home with someone of driving age had a car. In our family of five we had five cars or trucks. But cities are different, particularly higher density cities.

Most of my urban existence leading up to Vancouver was in auto-dominated suburbs in sprawling southwest desert cities (Phoenix and Tucson). While I began making changes to my lifestyle to incorporate more and more bicycling the low-density suburbs made it a bit more challenging. I would pedal four miles on a high-speed shoulderless road simply to get to a coffee shop. In Vancouver the decision not to have a car was basically made for us, but that didn't matter as we had to learn all of a sudden how to make it work. We soon realized that what was a "huge" lifestyle change for us was as normative for many in our neighborhood as Canadians loving hockey.

We lived in a higher-density neighborhood that was a prime landing place for international immigrants and refugees. As a result, many came from global megacities where they were already used to living in cramped spaces and using public transit. Our "noble" efforts to live car-free were met with, "So what?" It was during this time that I began diving deep into the world of transportation, equity, how cities are laid out and function, peak oil, and how so much of the built environment of our cities dictate and influence how we live on a daily basis. High-density cities like Manhattan or Tokyo dictate that most residents get around on transit, by foot, or by bicycle. Low-density cities like Phoenix or Houston dictate that most get around via the auto. Sure there are always exceptions to the rule, but so much of our urban existence really is dictated by the built environment. This is when and where we start getting into the conversation about equity and access to the kind of infrastructure needed to live and lead a bike-friendly or bike-oriented lifestyle.

This experience in Vancouver taught us that much of the transportation conversation really is about equity. Like many other immigrants and refugees we couldn't afford to drive a car and had to rely on transit and other forms of active transportation. However, our "loss" was really our gain as the lessons learned have forever stamped themselves on our lives. I don't view cars the same way any more (again, no conspiracy theories at play here) in the sense that I've come to realize owning an auto is *not* an American right. They are a privilege, and unfortunately it is the privileged who can afford to buy and use them. When we make cities, city services, and businesses accessible only to those who can afford to own a car, inequity begins rearing its ugly head.

I am on the streets daily in Portland on my bicycle. Most weeks I put on roughly a hundred miles. I see a lot, experience a lot, and observe a lot. Living in a central city neighborhood I have made this unfortunate observation ... *most* people pedaling on Portland streets are white. I know local and national organizations are scrambling and organizing in a hurry to rectify this; there is a greater push to get not only more minorities onto bikes, but women as well. I see the noble and laudable efforts of local organizations like the Community Cycling Center and national groups like People for Bikes or Red, Bike, and Green doing the necessary task of pointing out these realities and creatively addressing them. However, the sad truth is that the racial make-up remains lopsided not only in Portland, but in other cities as well.

So what?

Why care?

What's the big deal?

To me, as I've mentioned already, this boils down to a conversation about equity. This is the part of the book where I "play my cards" and let you into my world. You see, I've been a pastor and in vocational ministry all of my adult life since college. For me equity is not only a human rights conversation, but theological as well in that it is actually near and dear to the heart of God. While *The Bohemian Guide to Urban Cycling* is not a religious book, nor I am I subtly attempting to position it that way, it is all part of the combo deal of who I am ... this is the biggie fries and Coke that comes with the cheeseburger.

All of last year I worked on an urban sustainability project where I interacted with city leaders and academics from all over the country. In the beginning I always hid in my back pocket the fact that professionally I've been a minister. But the further one gets into the world of urban studies, urban renewal, redevelopment, gentrification, urban planning, and the like there emerges the poignant reality of the presence of urban churches across the country who've held together crumbling urban neighborhoods that were tumbling into blight, neglect, and degradation. I have read countless books and journal articles about the roles of these churches in partnering with city leaders to address the inequities plaguing their neighborhoods.

Slowly but surely I began pulling the "pastor card" out of my back pocket and started speaking freely when talking with city leaders, many of them were already partnering or talking with local churches and religious non-profits as they collectively sought the welfare and benefit of their cities. You see, we all want to see our cities thrive and to be places where equity and justice are upheld. We all simply go about it from different frameworks.

We all come from different perspectives. That adds color and variety to the topic and conversation about equity and bicycling in the city. Those different perspectives include feminist, non-religious, other faith traditions, gay, straight, right-wing, left-wing, chicken-wing, and so many more. Each perspective is a piece in the giant puzzle. I am humbled and appreciative of the collective voice of those who ride bikes who advocate for equity of access to biking as a mode of transportation and lifestyle regardless of their personal perspective. I simply cannot keep out of sight in my back pocket my own particular vantage point because it influences and shapes how I live and the way I approach this subject. For me it is the love and justness of God that propels me towards this end.

New York City pastor and *New York Times* best-selling author Tim Keller in his book *Generous Justice* begins by asserting, "Most people know that Jesus came to bring forgiveness and grace. Less well known is the Biblical teaching that a true experience of the grace of Jesus Christ inevitably motivates a man or woman to seek justice in the world."[1] One of the premises that Keller explores in the book is this notion that justice is not only an outflow of the nature and character of God, but its trickle-down effect, in that those who love and follow God are expected to do the same. This begins laying the foundation as to why churches have given themselves sacrificially to the betterment of their city through community development. But what really motivates churches? Is this notion of urban justice simply about doing good deeds or is there something deeper?

Keller points out that not only does justice originate in God, it is who God is, from which flows his concern for the poor, the vulnerable, the marginalized, the widow, the orphan, and the international immigrant. "If God's character includes a zeal for justice that leads him to have the tenderest love and closest involvement with the socially weak, then what should God's people be like?"[2] It can be argued that this same ethic and theological framework was woven into the DNA of the early church and which continued throughout the centuries. This is not meant to overlook or minimize the reality of those times throughout history where the church was and is corrupt and errant. But those moral lapses do not take away from God's initial call on the church to be a people marked by grace and justice.

---

[1] Keller, *Generous Justice,* ix.

[2] Ibid., 8.

Equity and bicycling are important topics to me on many fronts. Having lived at the bottom of the food chain while slugging it out to live life in the city I know firsthand the importance of getting around without a car. I know the reality of not being able to simply hop in a car to go for a cruise, to take the family to the beach, but instead to depend on transit to get groceries. I understand what it is like having a pull-along cart weighed down with groceries waiting for the next bus with two shivering cold and wet little children only to watch the bus simply pass by our stop. It was hard, and I was shocked to see how much it affected my identity, confidence, and the way I carried myself. And that was only for 18 months. What about those who know no other life? In that regard I am truly privileged beyond more than I can comprehend because at any time I could have "opted out," taken a good job in the States, and moved back home. Many don't have an "opt out" button to push.

I am white. I am middle-class. I am educated. I have one doctorate and am chipping away at a second. It can be argued that I do write from a position of power since I am in the majority. I don't say this out of *white guilt* but simply as an honest admission of where I stand. It was a painful and humbling experience living on so little, having to do most of our grocery shopping at the dollar store and buying most of our clothes at the thrift store. Not because it was a hipster thing to do, but because we simply didn't have a choice.

I push for and advocate more people getting out and bicycling in the city, because admittedly there is an appeal, a trendiness, and certainly a coolness factor to it. People outside of Portland who know and see me riding a singlespeed through the city streets (via social media) have a certain perception of this and I understand it. But I ride because I love to and I believe it is the most enjoyable, cost-efficient, and equitable forms of transportation (apart from walking).

Some people ride because it is the hipster thing to do. And do you know what? I'm fine with that. I'm actually happy more people are giving bicycling a chance regardless of motivation. On the other hand if we can build a more robust bicycle infrastructure in our cities that is both safe and accessible then more people will venture into bicycling as a mode of transportation because of the cost savings. Bike lanes don't cut it. We need separated bike facilities where we're comfortable taking an eight- and an eighty-year-old out on the streets. I thought about this a couple days ago when I was pedaling around Portland with my eleven-year-old. Once we got onto the neighborhood greenways we were fine and it was quite a relief once we did. But the one-mile stretch of bike lanes and riding alongside rumbling transit buses, fast-moving cars, and overall auto congestion was unnerving when it came to ensuring my son's safety.

There are multiple layers to this notion of equity and bicycling in the city. This ranges from education, advocacy, accessibility, to infrastructure. We can have great programs that educate anyone from school children to people living in urban ethnic enclaves, and we can have stellar programs to help get more bikes into peoples' hands, but if riding on the city streets is terrifying and nerve-wracking then people simply won't do it. They'll be loading up their bikes to drive to some separated trail next to some river or lake where they won't have to fear getting rear-ended or clipped by a passing car.

So how do we tackle the equity and bicycling issue and controversy, especially as it pertains to ethnic minorities and more marginalized populations? With that question posed let us first of all applaud and give a shout-out to all of the organizations, city governments, businesses, and individuals already laboriously rectifying this. With the proliferation of social media there is no shortage of good news of changes, victories, and progress towards more equity in bicycling. But let's take this momentum and build on it. What organization do you need to join? What advocacy group do you need to link arms with as a volunteer? Which citizen panel do you need to sit on? Which new non-profit do you need to start? Which innovation in the bicycling industry is bouncing around in the back of your mind that needs to become reality?

We can all play a part.

Your part will look different from my part.

Recently most of my work entails working with local churches in cities across North America teaching them about the changing dynamics of the city from urban renewal, gentrification, the creative class and the creative economy, to the impacts of active transportation (walkability and bikeability) on local churches. Much of my research and writing in the past year has been about encouraging churches to become more bikeable and bike-friendly. I have led a number of what I call *Bikeable Church Studios* in various cities teaching church leaders about reimagining their churches to focus on bikeability and being bike-friendly as part of seeking the welfare and betterment of their cities. One of the most exciting parts is that partnering with us in the studios are local city government leaders ranging from transportation planners to economic developers to non-profits to local bike-oriented businesses such as bike share and more.

There is a beauty to this kind of collaboration because a lot of churches have resonated with the ancient Hebrew writer Jeremiah who gave a charge to the Israelites who found themselves displaced in Babylon to "seek the welfare [or peace or prosperity] of the city." I have been in a number of meetings where there was an excitement among local city officials and employees upon learning that the church wanted to stand next to them and help make their cities more bikeable and bike-friendly whether through utilizing bike share more, adding more bike parking at churches and encouraging members to bike more, supporting new bicycle infrastructure initiatives, or simply advocating for a healthier and more sustainable transportation network in the city.

You see, we all can play a part regardless of our background, religious preference, political affiliations, sexual orientation, and so on. Access to equitable forms of transportation and infrastructure really is a human rights issue that can galvanize us to lay aside differences, link arms, and as a collective to seek the welfare of our cities whether for the poor or rich, white, black, or brown, urbanite or suburbanite, young or old, and everything in-between.

Central city neighborhoods are growing most quickly in terms of new bicycle infrastructure, but this also is synonymous with gentrification and urban infill. That means that those who need to be able to use bicycles as a mode of transportation are being displaced out farther from the city center where this kind of infrastructure is spotty at best. This does not minimize the need or importance of growing our bicycle facilities in the central city ... we need *more* not less. However, along with that we need more facilities in the *unsexy* parts of the cities where hipsters fear to tread, where there are no trendy brewpubs or coffee roasters. These are the places that continue to be the catch-basin for the displaced urban poor. Obviously every city looks different in this regard, but you get the point. We need better bike facilities in parts of the city and among population segments that would most benefit from them.

However, as I briefly touched on before, this also entails more than bike lanes or (hopefully) separated cycle tracks. It's a package deal involving education, advocacy, and the like. We all can play a role in our cities and communities in pushing for equity in bicycling. Let's roll up our sleeves and jump in!

Sean Benesh

Chapter 13

Perspective

Admittedly I'm a mountain biker first and an urban cyclist second (at least I am today). I cannot deny that fact and reality even though I love cities more than the wilderness. My own life has gone through a lot of tweaks, changes, and adaptations along the way. As much as I'm a city-first kind of guy, I still love the sport, life, culture, and vibe of mountain biking ... enduro, cross country, downhill, cyclocross, and more.

For many years through college and grad school I pined for the wilderness areas. Later on I worked as a mountain biking guide and my life seemed to revolve around getting out into the backcountry. I was on the trail mountain biking, hiking, or exploring almost every day of the week. On weekends we would have "Daddy's Big Day" where I'd whisk the family away to some remote wilderness area in SE Arizona. We'd explore ancient Hohokam villages, old mammoth kill sites that had been excavated, or stroll through high-elevation alpine meadows in the mountains above the desert floor. In a 1995 Chevy Suburban with a 42-gallon gas tank we'd drive all over the desert and mountains looking for new and exciting places to explore as we learned about the wilderness areas. But that all began to change ...

I started a doctoral program that in essence looked at global cities and the impacts of urbanization and the re-orientation of cities. Part of my coursework was in China where we went on a three-city tour meeting with NGOs, university faculty, and government leaders to discuss the implications of urbanization in China. Much of the conversation centered around the role of NGOs and churches in their humanitarian efforts among the marginalized populations. My world became immersed in reading and writing about all things *urban*.

I began spending more time rediscovering Tucson in light of what I was learning within this new framework. I was thrust into a new epoch where I began distancing myself from my "former" life as a mountain biking guide. Instead of pouring over topographical maps, trail guide books, mountain bike magazines and the like I was reading about gentrification, urban renewal projects, and a massive amount of online material detailing Tucson's attempt to revitalize its downtown. Sure, I still went mountain biking on occasion, but I found myself more and more going to the gym to work out. My love for the great wilderness areas and the blank spots on the map was diminishing with my growing love and passion to understand cities. It was an exchange of the rural wilderness for the urban jungle which captivated me as much, if not more, than discovering a previously unfound Hohokam village site off the beaten path.

But I could never shake my love for mountain biking. I chafed (literally and figuratively) under the idea of being a true roadie and urban cycling guy. Besides, as I've mentioned numerous times before, I don't do well with skin-tight Lycra. But as time passed my once-beloved singlespeed mountain bike began showing signs of age and distress due to neglect. After relocating to the Pacific Northwest a few spots of rust showed up on its frame and my components quickly became obsolete (what little there were). To top it all off I even had changed my Twitter handle. I dropped "mtbikerguy" and went with plain old "seanbenesh." I even began looking at the surrounding mountains with a bit of disdain as I was all about the city, urban living, and favoring walkable cities, densifying central cities, and urban culture. I just didn't see how mountain biking fit in.

And then I woke up ...

It wasn't quite like when Neo wakes up in a future reality in *The Matrix*, but there certainly was for me a rebirth process. I had struggled to hold in tension my love for high-density complex cities with bombing down a pristine singletrack on some remote mountain ridge. I guess I worried that I'd go back to my former ways of avoiding cities and being fretful of them as I had been when I was a mountain biking guide. But it didn't happen.

The best part? My love for all things *urban* or *city* did not diminish ... instead I figured out how to embrace the best of both worlds. I'm one of those types that goes "all in" on things. I don't do anything half-hearted which meant my plunge into studying, understanding, and living in the city was more than feet first ... it was all encompassing. I couldn't hold in tension my love for mountain biking, the wilderness, and still at the same time be a passionate advocate for healthy and sustainable cities and urban living.

So I dusted off my mountain bike, pumped the tires back up, re-lubed everything and began riding again ... and again ... and again ... and again. Not only that, but due to years of neglect I fully upgraded my beloved singlespeed with new components, a new wheelset, and a sweet new "enduro blue" paint job. I was and am "back." But back in a new and different way. I'm a guy who loves everything about bicycles. On the one hand I love, affirm, and appreciate mountain biking and the community that goes with it. At the same time, I truly am an urban cyclist now. I actually spend more time pedaling around the streets of Portland than I do on trails like Post Canyon or Syncline in the Gorge. I love and do both and it provides a balance for me.

Maybe it is that I'm getting older but balance is something I rarely had previously. The only time I was centered was when the pendulum was swinging from one extreme to the other. My boys have listened to me extol the virtues of cities, multiculturalism, density, the creative economy and class, urban innovation, agglomeration economies, suburban angst, bicycling in the city, bike commuting, and the like ... but I also take them mountain biking. "Daddy's Big Day" has taken new twists and turns as I have pieced together, built, and bought more mountain bikes so we can all go riding together.

I also view as complimentary my love for reading *Urban Velo* magazine which plunges me into the urban cycling world of fixies, bike polo, skinny jeans, and sweet mustaches alongside *Bike* and *Enduro* magazines which are all about mountain biking. I have reclaimed my "mtbikerguy" Twitter handle and connect with many more mountain bikers.

But where is this conversation leading? What does this have to do with a book on urban cycling?

From all of my studies, teaching opportunities, and writings, one thing that has surfaced continuously is the theme of justice and equity that I addressed in the previous chapter. The bottom line is that I'm in favor of getting *more* people on bicycles whether they become Lycra-clad roadies, baggie-clothed enduro mountain bikers, nutty cyclocross racers, moms on cargo bikes, skinny jeans-wearing hipsters on fixies, Portlandy tall-bike clowns, Darth Vader in a kilt riding a unicycle playing the bagpipes, M.A.M.I.L.s, or kids with Wal-mart fat bikes ... it doesn't really matter. What really matters is that more people hop on bikes and begin using them as a way of life and a mode of transportation.

Yesterday I walked into Velo Cult bike shop to order some coffee (yes, this bike shop serves locally roasted coffee and beers) and the mechanic / barista / bartender was working on a bicycle that I could tell was from the mid-1990s. It was (to me) an OK-looking bike and I didn't much care for the color scheme. I couldn't immediately tell what brand it was and I didn't think anything of it. As I chatted with the mechanic I soon learned that this city commuter / touring bike was a highly coveted bike that'll set you back about $4,000. "Meh," I thought to myself.

It's not that I don't like nice bikes (because I do!) I just think about the bare essentials of bicycling as a mode of transportation. Who really cares what we look like when we bike over to a coffee shop, brew pub, or to work? But then again I am being hypocritical because I do love my bike and even though I went on the cheap I have labored over assembling the right components and color scheme to go for the "look" that I desire. OK, guilty as charged, but my bike is merely a fraction of a $4,000 bike. But what is this conversation really about?

One of the concepts that I have tried to flesh out throughout this book, especially as I write about different kinds of bikes for urban life, is that one of the most overlooked "kinds" of bikes are simply those that roll. Period. Again, I like bikes and I enjoy the beauty and craftsmanship of custom bikes. I have fawned over bikes that I knew cost $15,000 and those "down" to $4,000. But at the end of the day the most basic ingredient is we need to get more people on bikes regardless of which kind they choose. There is a certain level of freedom in picking up a bike that is utilitarian and nothing more than that.

I recently came across a bike company that purposely made inexpensive commuter bikes. I love the fact that on their (now defunct) website they came right out and say, "We try to make our bikes easy to use, low maintenance and inexpensive. We believe if we do that, you will want to ride them more." Since the cost of bicycling is the bike itself the most important thing is to be able to get more people onto bikes in the city. For that reason, while I love and affirm custom bike builders and appreciate what they bring to the industry, I also have to admit most often I tip my hat at bike companies that are making biking more accessible to a greater number of people. Let's lower the barriers inhibiting people from getting out and bicycling as a way of life and mode of transportation in the city.

This mountain biker's take on the whole urban cycling scene is that I'm stoked to see more people on bikes. Let's simply get out and ride. For those with the cabbage to buy higher-end bikes, whether for the road or for off-road trails, or those who scrape by getting a cheap utilitarian bike, the great equalizer is that we simply are unified in this one aspect ... we ride ... and we ride *together*. Let us remember to keep this main thing about bicycling the main thing.

Sean Benesh

Afterword

Yesterday I led a bicycling tour through the city. It was for a group of students from a small rural college in the Midwest. They literally transitioned from getting off the plane to dropping into downtown Portland and hopping onto bikes. For most it was both a bit disorienting as well as the best way to acclimatize themselves to Portland. As we pedaled through various districts around downtown—the Pearl, eastside industrial district, and more—I was reminded of a number of recent blogs, social media rants, and articles about Portland's struggle to not only maintain our beloved status as "America's Bicycle Capital," but to aggressively put in bike facilities that would make non-aggressive and unconfident bicyclists feel confident riding in the city.

Having taken hundreds of people on city tours I am always a little nervous ... nervous for the participants, especially those who are not used to biking around an urban environment or whose bike skills are suspect. It reminds me again and again of the need and importance for robust facilities that encourage *more* people to hop in the saddle and give urban cycling a whirl. For the vast majority of people I've taken on tours I wonder out loud how many of them would venture onto these same roads without someone leading them and wooing them on? How many would feel confident taking the lane, especially during rush hour where cyclists get crowded over to the curb due to a lack of bike lanes or, if there are bike facilities, to confidently ride alongside people rushing around in two-thousand pound masses of steel hoping to get home before the next guy or gal?

What is commonplace after a bike tour wraps up is there is a real sense of elation from participants. A growing confidence that they tackled the behemoth of actually riding in the city next to Portland hipsters and other M.A.M.I.L.s. Not only that, but they learned that they could indeed navigate through the downtown core and get around without the hassle of being stuck in traffic or the ease of pulling up to Water Avenue Coffee across the Willamette to simply lock a bike out front and walk in while not fretting about finding parking spots. It is truly easy to get around the city on a bike. But many simply lack the confidence and experience or know-how to jump in without help ... or a push ... or an enticement.

How can we woo and entice people to get out of their cars and take to the streets on a bike? What is my role? What is your role?

Bibliography

Andersen, Michael. "How Economic Growth Sold Portland
   Landlords on a Bikeway." *People for Bikes*, January 6, 2013.
   Online: http://www.peopleforbikes.org/blog/entry/how-
   economic-growth-sold-portland-landlords-on-a-bikeway.
_____. "Good Bike Access Helps Score Great
   Workers, Portland Firms Say." *People for Bikes*, January 21,
   2013. Online: http://www.peopleforbikes.org/blog/entry/
   good-bike-access-helps-score-great-workers-portland-
   firms-say.
_____. "Portland Retailers Swoop Into Storefronts
   Along Bikeways." *People for Bikes*, March 4, 2013. Online:
   http://www.peopleforbikes.org/blog/entry/portland-
   retailers-swoop-into-storefronts-along-bikeways.
_____. "3 Reasons Portland Retailers Have
   Embraced Bike Parking." *People for Bikes*, April 24, 2013.
   Online: http://www.peopleforbikes.org/blog/entry/3-
   reasons-Portland-retailers-have-embraced-bike-parking.
_____. "Low-car households account for 60% of
   Portland's growth since 2005." *BikePortland*, July 30, 2013.
   Online: http://bikeportland.org/2013/07/30/low-car-
   households-account-for-60-of-portland-growth-
   since-2005-91282.
_____. "Streets with Scarce Auto Parking Are the
   Best to Remove Auto Parking." *People for Bikes*,
   September 11, 2013. Online: http://

www.peopleforbikes.org/blog/entry/streets-with-scarce-
auto-parking-are-the-best-places-to-remove-auto-
parking.

_____. "Here are the 4 Ways Protected Bike Lanes
Help Local Businesses." *People for Bikes*, September 16,
2013. Online: http://www.peopleforbikes.org/blog/entry/
here-are-the-4-ways-protected-bike-lanes-help-local-
businesses.

Baker, Linda. "Developers Cater to Two-Wheeled Traffic in
Portland, Ore." *New York Times*, September 20, 2011.
Online: http://www.nytimes.com/2011/09/21/business/
portland-ore-developments-cater-to-bicycle-riders.html?
pagewanted=all&_r=1&.

Brugmann, Jeb. *Welcome to the Urban Revolution: How Cities
are Changing the World.* Toronto: Viking Canada, 2009.

City Club of Portland. "Case Study: North Williams Avenue."
Online: http://pdxcityclub.org/2013/Report/Portland-
Bicycle-Transit/2013/Report/Case-Study-North-
Williams-Avenue.

Clifton, K., et al. "Catering to the Bicycling Market." *TR News*
280 (2012) 26-32.

Clifton, K. *Examining Consumer Behavior and Travel Choices.*
Portland: Portland State University, 2013.

Crain, Liz. "Portland's North Williams Avenue." *Via
Magazine,* July/August 2011. Online: http://
www.viamagazine.com/destinations/portlands-north-
williams-avenue.

Flanagan, William G. *Urban Sociology: Images and Structure.*
Lanham: Rowman & Littlefield, 2010.

Florida, Richard. *The Rise of the Creative Class: And How It's
Transforming Work, Leisure, Community and Everyday Life.*
New York: Basic, 2004.

_____. *Who's Your City?: How the Creative Economy
is Making Where We Live the Most Important Decision of
Your Life.* New York: Basic, 2008.

Gibson, Karen J. "Bleeding Albina: A History of Community Disinvestment, 1940-2000." *Transforming Anthropology* 15:1 (2007) 3-25.

Glaeser, Edward L. *Triumph of the City: How Our Greatest Invention Makes Us Richer, Smarter, Greener, Healthier, and Happier.* New York: Penguin, 2011.

Goodyear, Sarah. "Bike Lane Backlash, Even in Portland." *The Atlantic Cities,* September 20, 2011. Online: http://www.theatlanticcities.com/neighborhoods/2011/09/portland-bike-lanes-open-racial-wounds/138/.

———. "The Trendification of Brooklyn and the Perils of a Successful Urban Brand." *The Atlantic Cities,* August 16, 2012. Online: http://www.theatlanticcities.com/neighborhoods/2012/08/trendification-brooklyn-and-perils-successful-urban-brand/2973/.

———. "The Surprising Diversity of the America Cycling Community." *The Atlantic Cities,* May 29, 2013. Online: http://www.theatlanticcities.com/commute/2013/05/surprising-diversity-american-cycling-community/5737/.

Greenfield, John. "Bike facilities don't have to be 'the white lanes of gentrification.'" *Grid Chicago,* May 10, 2012. Online: http://gridchicago.com/2012/bike-facilities-dont-have-to-be-the-white-lanes-of-gentrification/.

Harper, Douglas. "Bohemian." *Online Etymology Dictionary.* Online: http://www.etymonline.com/index.php?term=bohemian&allowed_in_frame=0.

Heying, Charles. *Brew to Bikes: Portland's Artisan Economy.* Portland: Ooligan, 2010.

Hiller, Harry H. *Urban Canada.* New York: Oxford University Press, 2009.

Keller, Timothy. *Generous Justice: How God's Grace Makes Us Just.* New York: Riverhead, 2012.

Lee, A. "What is the Economic Contribution of Cyclists Compared to Car Drivers in Inner Suburban Melbourne's

Shopping Strips?" Masters' thesis. The University of
Melbourne, Melbourne, 2008.

Lees, Loretta, et al. *Gentrification.* New York: Routledge, 2007.

LeGates, Richard T., and Frederic Stout. *The City Reader.* New
York: Routledge, 2011.

Lloyd, Richard. *Neo-Bohemia: Art and Commerce in the
Postindustrial City.* New York: Routledge, 2010.

Loving, Lisa. "Portland Gentrification: The North Williams
Avenue That Was–1956." *The Scanner*, August 9, 2011.
Online: http://theskanner.com/article/Portland-
Gentrification-The-North-Williams-Avenue-That-
Was--1956-2011-08-09.

Manning, Ivy. "Explore Portland's North William's Avenue."
Sunset Magazine. Online: http://www.sunset.com/travel/
northwest/portland-north-williams-00400000038096/.
_____. "Go Green on Portland's North Williams."
Sunset Magazine. Online: http://www.sunset.com/travel/
northwest/portland-day-trip-00400000038083/.

Magnuson, Mike. *Bike Tribes: A Field Guide to North American
Cyclists.* New York: Rodale, 2012.

Maus, Jonathan. "Meeting on Williams project turns into
discussion of race, gentrification." *BikePortland*, July 21,
2011. Online: http://bikeportland.org/2011/07/21/
racism-rears-its-head-on-williams-project-56633?
utm_source=feedburner&utm_medium=feed&utm_camp
aign=Feed%3A+BikePortland+%28BikePortland.org%29.
_____. "New Seasons makes bike access a top
priority at new Williams Ave location." *BikePortland*,
March 27, 2013. Online: http://bikeportland.org/
2013/03/27/new-seasons-makes-bike-access-a-top-
priority-at-new-williams-ave-location-84690.

Navas, Melissa. "North Williams traffic safety plan gives
neighbors a chance to delve into deeper issues of race,
gentrification." *Oregon Live*, August 11, 2011. Online:
http://www.oregonlive.com/portland/index.ssf/2011/08/
north_williams_traffic_safety.html.

Portland Bureau of Transportation. "Bicycle Parking Corrals." *The City of Portland Oregon*. Online: https://www.portlandoregon.gov/transportation/article/250076.

Pucher, John and Ralph Buehler. *City Cycling*. Cambridge: MIT Press, 2012

Recinos, H.J. "Racism and Drugs in the City: The Church's Call to Ministry." In *Envisioning the New City: A Reader on Urban Ministry*, edited by Eleanor Scott Meyers, 98-108. Louisville: Westminster/John Knox, 1992.

Smith, Rob. "This isn't the North Williams Avenue I remember." *Portland Business Journal*, April 3, 2013. Online: http://www.bizjournals.com/portland/blog/real-estate-daily/2013/04/this-isnt-the-north-williams-avenue-i.html.

Snyder, Tanya. "Cyclists of Color: Invisible No More." *DC Streets Blog*, May 29, 2013. Online: http://dc.streetsblog.org/2013/05/29/cyclists-of-color-invisible-no-more/.

Speck, Jeff. *Walkable City: How Downtown Can Save America, One Step at a Time*. New York: North Point, 2012.

Urban Dictionary LLC, "bohemian." *Urban Dictionary*. Online: http://www.urbandictionary.com/define.php?term=bohemian.

Wikimedia Foundation Inc., "Bohemianism." *Wikipedia*. Online: http://en.wikipedia.org/wiki/Bohemianism.

Wilson, William J. "From Institutional to Jobless Ghettos." In *The City Reader*, edited by Richard T. LeGates & Frederic Stout, 117-126. New York: Routledge, 2011.

Zukin, Sharon. "The Creation of a 'Loft Lifestyle.'" In *The Gentrification Debates*, edited by Japonica Brown-Saracino, 175-184. New York: Routledge, 2010.

_____. *Naked City The Death and Life of Authentic Urban Places*. New York: Oxford University Press, 2011.

About the Author

Sean Benesh lives in Portland, Oregon. He has experience as a mountain biking, hiking, and urban cycling guide in Arizona and Oregon. Everything that Sean rides is a singlespeed whether on the road or on the dirt. Gears are overrated ... When not on the trail or zipping through the streets of Portland on his bike, you'll find him hunkered down in a coffee shop reading and writing. Sean completed his doctorate focusing on urban studies with attention given to faith-based non-profit community development in gentrifying neighborhoods. You can connect with him at @mtbikerguy or www.seanbenesh.com.

About Urban Loft Publishers

Urban Loft Publishers focuses on ideas, topics, themes, and conversations about all things urban. Renewing the city is the central theme and focus of what we publish. It is our intention to blend urban ministry, theology, urban planning, architecture, urbanism, stories, and the social sciences, as ways to drive the conversation. While we lean towards scholarly and academic works, we explore the fun and lighter sides of cities as well. We publish a wide variety of urban perspectives, from books by the experts *about* the city to personal stories and personal accounts of urbanites who *live* in the city.

CPSIA information can be obtained
at www.ICGtesting.com
Printed in the USA
LVHW081834021219
639178LV00045B/4195/P